"VOLUME ONE"

Thoughts on Spirituality

Direction for Our Times
As given to "Anne,"
a lay apostle

"VOLUME ONE"

Direction for Our Times
As given to "Anne," a lay apostle

ISBN-13: 978-0-9766841-0-7
ISBN-10: 0-9766841-0-1

Library of Congress Number: Applied For

© Copyright 2004 Direction for Our Times.
All rights reserved. Revised Edition 2006.

Publisher:
Direction for Our Times
9000 West 81st Street
Justice, IL 60458
708-496-9300
www.directionforourtimes.com

Direction for Our Times is a 501(c)(3) tax-exempt organization.

Manufactured in the United States of America

Graphic Design: Pete Massari

How to Pray the Rosary information and the image of Our Lady Immaculate are used with permission. Copyright © Congregation of Marians of the Immaculate Conception, Stockbridge, MA 01263. www.marian.org.

Copy of painting of *Jesus Christ the Returning King* by Janusz Antosz, reproduced with permission.

Dear Friends,

I am very much impressed with the messages delivered by Anne who states that they are received from God the Father, Jesus, and the Blessed Mother. They provide material for excellent and substantial meditation for those to whom they are intended, namely to the laity, to bishops and priests; and sinners with particular difficulties. These messages should not be read hurriedly but reserved for a time when heartfelt recollection and examination can be made.

I am impressed by the complete dedication of Anne to the authority of the magisterium, to her local Bishop and especially to the Holy Father. She is a very loyal daughter of the Church.

Sincerely in Christ,

Philip M. Hannan

Archbishop Philip M. Hannan, (Ret.)
President of FOCUS Worldwide Network
Retired Archbishop of New Orleans

PMH/aac

Without in any way seeking to anticipate the final and definitive judgment of the local bishop and of the Holy See (to which we owe our filial obedience of mind and heart), I wish to manifest my personal discernment concerning the nature of the messages received by "Anne," a Lay Apostle.

After an examination of the reported messages and an interview with the visionary herself, I personally believe that the messages received by "Anne" are of supernatural origin.

The message contents are in conformity with the faith and morals teachings of the Catholic Church's Magisterium and in no way violate orthodox Catholic doctrine. The phenomena of the precise manner of how the messages are transmitted (i.e., the locutions and visions) are consistent with the Church's historical precedence for authentic private revelation. The spiritual fruits (cf. Mt. 12:33) of Christian faith, conversion, love, and interior peace, based particularly upon a renewed awareness of the indwelling Christ and prayer before the Blessed Sacrament, have been significantly manifested in various parts of the world within a relatively brief time since the messages have been received and promulgated. Hence the principal criteria used by ecclesiastical commissions to investigate reported supernatural events (message, phenomena, and spiritual fruits) are, in my opinion, substantially satisfied in the case of "Anne's" experience.

The messages which speak of the coming of Jesus Christ, the "Returning King" do not refer to an imminent end of the world with Christ's final physical coming, but rather call for a spiritual receptivity to an ongoing spiritual return of Jesus Christ, a dynamic advent of Jesus which ushers in a time of extraordinary grace and peace for humanity (in ways similar to the Fatima promise for an eventual era of peace as a result of the Triumph of the Immaculate Heart of Mary, or perhaps the "new springtime" for the Church referred to by the words of the great John Paul II).

As "Anne" has received permission from her local ordinary, Bishop Leo O'Reilly, for the spreading of her messages, and has also submitted all her writings to the Congregation for the Doctrine of the Faith, I would personally encourage, (as the Church herself permits), the prayerful reading of these messages, as they have constituted an authentic spiritual benefit for a significant number of Catholic leaders throughout the world.

Dr. Mark Miravalle
Professor of Theology and Mariology
Franciscan University of Steubenville
October 13, 2006

Table of Contents

Introduction

Dear Reader,

I am a wife, mother of six, and a Secular Franciscan.

At the age of twenty, I was divorced for serious reasons and with pastoral support in this decision. In my mid-twenties I was a single parent, working and bringing up a daughter. As a daily Mass communicant, I saw my faith as sustaining and had begun a journey toward unity with Jesus, through the Secular Franciscan Order or Third Order.

My sister travelled to Medjugorje and came home on fire with the Holy Spirit. After hearing of her beautiful pilgrimage, I experienced an even more profound conversion. During the following year I experienced various levels of deepened prayer, including a dream of the Blessed Mother, where she asked me if I would work for Christ. During the dream she showed me that this special spiritual work would mean I would be separated from others in the world. She actually showed me my extended family and how I would be separated from them. I told her that I did not care. I would do anything asked of me.

Shortly after, I became sick with endometriosis. I have been sick ever since, with one thing or another. My sicknesses are always the types that mystify doctors in the beginning. This is part of the cross and I mention it because so many suffer in this way. I was told by my doctor that I would never conceive children. As a single parent, this did not concern me as I assumed it was God's will. Soon after, I met a wonderful man. My first marriage had been annulled and we married and conceived five children.

Spiritually speaking, I had many experiences that included what I now know to be interior locutions. These moments were beautiful and the words still stand out firmly in my heart, but I did not get excited because I was busy offering up illnesses and exhaustion. I took it as a matter of course that Jesus had to work hard to sustain me as He had given me a lot to handle. In looking back, I see that He was preparing me to do His work. My preparation period was long, difficult and not very exciting. From the outside, I think people thought, "Man, that woman has bad luck." From the inside, I saw that while my sufferings were painful and long lasting, my little family was growing in love, in size and in wisdom, in the sense that my husband and I certainly understood what was important and what was not important. Our continued crosses did that for us.

Various circumstances compelled my husband and me to move with our children far from my loved ones. I offered this up and must say it is the most difficult thing I have had to contend with. Living in exile brings many beautiful opportunities to align with Christ's will; however, you have to continually remind yourself that you are doing that. Otherwise you just feel sad. After several years in exile, I finally got the inspiration to go to Medjugorje. It was actually a gift from my husband for my fortieth birthday. I had tried to go once before, but circumstances prevented the trip and I understood it was not God's will. Finally, though, it was time and my eldest daughter and I found ourselves in front of St. James church. It was her second trip to Medjugorje.

I did not expect or consider that I would experience anything out of the ordinary. My daughter, who loved it on her first trip, made many jokes about people looking for miracles. She affectionately calls Medjugorje a carnival for religious people. She also says it is the happiest place on earth. This young woman initially went there as a rebellious fourteen-year-old, who took the opportunity to travel abroad with her aunt. She returned calm and respectful, prompting my husband to say we would send all our teenagers on pilgrimage.

At any rate, we had a beautiful five days. I experienced a spiritual healing on the mountain. My daughter rested and prayed. A quiet but significant thing happened to me. During my Communions, I spoke with Jesus conversationally. I thought this was beautiful, but it had happened before on occasion so I was not stunned or overcome. I remember telling others that Communions in Medjugorje were powerful. I came home, deeply grateful to Our Lady for bringing us there.

The conversations continued all that winter. At some time in the six months that followed our trip, the conversations leaked into my life and came at odd times throughout the day. Jesus began to direct me with decision and I found it more and more difficult to refuse when He asked me to do this or that. I told no one.

During this time, I also began to experience direction from the Blessed Mother. Their voices are not hard to distinguish. I do not hear them in an auditory way, but in my soul or mind. By this time I knew that something remarkable was occurring and Jesus was telling me that He had special work for me, over and above my primary vocation as wife and mother. He told me to write the messages down and that He would arrange to have them published and disseminated. Looking back, it took Him a long time to get me comfortable enough where I was willing to trust Him. I trust His voice now and will continue to do my best to serve Him, given my constant struggle with weaknesses, faults, and the pull of the world.

Please pray for me as I continue to try to serve Jesus. Please answer "yes" to Him because He so badly needs us and He is so kind. He will take you right into His heart if you let Him. I am praying for you and am so grateful to God that He has given you these words. Anyone who knows Him must fall in love with Him, such is His goodness. If you have been struggling, this is your answer. He is coming to you in a special way through these words and the graces that flow through them.

Please do not fall into the trap of thinking that He cannot possibly mean for you to reach high levels of holiness. As I say somewhere in my writings, the greatest sign of the times is Jesus having to make do with the likes of me as His secretary. I consider myself the B-team, dear friends. Join me and together we will do our little bit for Him.

Message received from Jesus immediately following my writing of the above biographical information:

You see, My child, that you and I have been together for a long time. I was working quietly in your life for years before you began this work. Anne, how I love you. You can look back through your life and see so many "yes" answers to Me. Does that not please you and make you glad? You began to say "yes" to Me long before you experienced extraordinary graces. If you had not, My dearest, I could never have given you the graces or assigned this mission to you. Do you see how important it was that you got up every day, in your ordinary life, and said "yes" to your God, despite difficulty, temptation, and hardship? You could not see the big plan as I saw it. You had to rely on your faith. Anne, I tell you today, it is still that way. You cannot see My plan, which is bigger than your human mind can accept. Please continue to rely on your faith as it brings Me such glory. Look at how much I have been able to do with you, simply because you made a quiet and humble decision for Me. Make another quiet and humble decision on this day and every day, saying, "I will serve God." Last night you served Me by bringing comfort to a soul in pain. You decided against yourself and for Me, through your service to him. There was gladness in heaven, Anne. You are Mine. I am yours. Stay with Me, My child. Stay with Me.

Prayers to God, The Eternal Father

Dear God in Heaven, I pledge my allegiance to You. I give You my life, my work, and my heart. In turn, give me the grace of obeying Your every direction to the fullest possible extent. Amen.

God my Father, help me to understand. Amen.

Thoughts
on Spirituality

–1–

Thoughts on Spirituality

Jesus said: *"I did not come to you because you were worthy. I won't leave you because you are not."*

This morning I went to Mass. It has been a particularly difficult time, with unrest, stressful business situations, and acrimonious discussions between my husband and I. This follows a tremendously hard Lent. I went into church and glanced over at the First Station of the Cross, thinking of the Lent I had just suffered through and commenting to Jesus, sarcastically, that it was too soon to pack away the Stations of the Cross. This was met with peaceful silence. I threw up various other "feel sorry for me" comments. No comments came back.

Beginning to feel like the complainer I was, I received Communion. Jesus began to speak, telling me I was like a child riding a bicycle for the first time. He, like any good parent, was running along behind me. He let me go for a minute. Actually, it was a day and a half. This was for my benefit, to give me practice at keeping my spiritual balance. He had never left me and would not have let me ride into dangerous areas. He was with me all along. This thought caused me to cringe, thinking of the last day and a half and my not-so-peaceful responses to various stressors and difficulties. Yes, He had heard the swear words.

Back to the bike. He would not have let me fall, even though I had felt like I was falling. I began to fall, I think, and He caught me. The sensation of losing my balance and danger had frightened me. Like any wobbly child, I don't want to be let go of. Not even for a moment. He assured me I was loved, indeed cherished, and that He wouldn't leave me to myself again for some time. I said churlishly, "So I failed the test." He replied, *"It was not a test. It was practice. And you did not fail. You practiced. I am with you. I am teaching you. And you are learning. Be joyful. I will never leave you."*

"Be on my side, the side of peace."

My heart aches. I love Jesus so much that it is difficult to *only* communicate with Him in this way. I want to be with Him. The suffering can be dreadful. I don't like it. I'm not a sufferer. But the longing for Jesus, while an ache, is one I would not trade. I want it to become even more intense. I don't understand completely what is happening. Or why it is happening. I spent nearly a year being afraid because I was so unworthy. He assured me that He does not make mistakes and that He knows me and chose to come to me in this way for reasons, primarily, to prepare me to do His work. I can be comfortable in my unworthiness, as long as I am doing my best. Now this seems simple and a simple thought. It was only Father who set me free of that awful feeling of trepidation. I feared it was in my

imagination or worse, some sort of demonic interference. I trusted Jesus all along, and trusted the
Blessed Mother to protect me. Let me say that at no
time did I feel tremendous anxiety. I felt peaceful,
but bemused.

Father told me, after praying over me, that "Your
gift is no illusion. Jesus is with you. He is calling on
you to live the interior life as a mother and wife. He
also wants you to do something with your hands
for Him. What do you do with your hands?" I told
him I wrote. He nodded and smiled. "That's it, of
course. I should have known. He wants you to write
with Him and for Him." This filled me with untold
joy and relief, because this is what I was getting
from Jesus, and frankly I was happy to know I was
not imagining things. He also instructed me to do a
scriptural office every morning, which is a pre-
determined set of readings. He told me that my con-
fusion was arising because, in an attempt to respond
to this special gift, I had been reading various
saints, as I always have, but more seriously since
the communications began. He told me that the
saints I was attempting to emulate had lived in
monasteries and convents, while I was called upon
to live in the world and in the home. Hence the con-
fusion. I had walked around feeling guilty 24 hours
a day because I was failing, when really, in doing
my duty united to my Jesus, I was serving Him
according to His precious will. Father put me on a
beautiful, holy, and confident path. My scriptural
prayer is powerful, rich, and revealing. Jesus leaves

nothing to chance with me. He tells me when to work on my book, which is after the house needs are met and my daily prayers are said.

One day I began to work, having forgotten to pray. He stopped me and said, *"Pray."*

I tried to shake Him off as I was delayed to begin with. The word came again. *"Pray. Your work must be Mine. To do that, you must start with Me."*

Of course I did, and received such joy and comfort that I began to write with a light and happy heart. He instructs me in this way, often telling me when to be quiet, or when not to make a call. I wish He would tell me when to stop swearing but I suppose it's such a given He puts His fingers in His ears and tries not to roll His eyes. I felt His exasperation this morning when I said, "So I failed." If He wasn't Jesus, He would have rolled His eyes. But His patience is boundless, thanks be to God, our Father. I rely on His patience. I depend on it, and abuse it daily.

On His timing, I finished a rough draft on the morning the children got out of school for Easter break. He conveyed to me that I was not to work on it again until they were back in school. My duty for those ten days was with the children. I put it away but at one point considered picking it up and reading through it. *"No,"* was the answer. *"This small thing is a mortification. Leave it alone until it is time."* I realize that obedience is paramount and did as I was told. I try to obey in other things.

During fights with my husband He often tells me, *"Leave him to Me."* I'm not as obedient there, as He works a bit slower than I like when it comes to bringing the husband around. And how can I be sure the husband is listening when Jesus talks? Perhaps he mightn't pay attention as closely as I do, therefore I tell the husband what I think God wants him to know, loudly, in case he's not listening. This does not please God and I have to work on it.

God does not want me to smoke again. My love affair with cigarettes ended 7 years ago but I still pick them up the odd time. During my last put them down and walk away decision, I prayed in front of the tabernacle.

Jesus said, *"Would you blow smoke into this tabernacle? I am with you, inside you. You carry Me with you. Do not smoke."*

This was not an ambivalent message and I didn't smoke after that, although I think about it every day.

Jesus often wants me to get out of His way so He can work with someone, perhaps someone I am speaking to. I understand at times this is happening and try to quiet my soul so He can use me to speak to a person who might be struggling. I love writing with Christ. It just happens, and flows. It's flowing now and I don't feel the work of it. I love Jesus and during the most difficult times of Lent feel a nearly physical sense of realigning my will to His, despite the most horrid spiritual afflictions, and angst. There is nothing else for me anymore. The world holds little solace. Often there is no comfort to be found anymore on this earth. No person can console me. Nothing. No food, no comfort. I am alone in a crowd, even of like minded souls. It's dreadful to experience but the fruit is a spiritual leading with your chin kind of feeling or stepping out into the darkness with faith. It does toughen you and I can see that now. I hate it, make no mistake. The people around me must benefit, though, from this proximity of mine to Christ. I am afraid that through the suffering I will be unable to complete my duties at times. But no, He gives me that. He sees to the details in the most remarkable of ways. I cannot fault Him, and as I say, there is nothing else but Him. I rely on Him for everything.

One more thought for today. Sister has often told me I should record some of the thoughts or experiences. Sister lives in Community nearby and is a dear friend and advisor to me. Writing, which I see as work, comes easily but there was a small part of me that thought, "Oh, so now You want me to do this, in addition to everything else?" (How does He stand me?) So in the spirit of wanting a personal invitation, I refused to write.

I once asked Him outright and He said, ***"The time***

will come. It is not now." After one lovely experience I said, "Hey God, maybe I should be writing this stuff down." He smiled and gave me to know without words that that is usually how He completes His will in us. He didn't want me to begin a spiritual journal with a bad attitude. So He gave me the desire to do it. He gave me a burning need to transcribe these interactions. In other words, why resist? He'll get His way and I live for His will so I should stop complaining. Still I hesitated, being engrossed with my other work. Sister this morning asked me to begin to chronicle the experiences and frankly, when Sister talks, I listen and treat everything she says as something I must obey. She is a lovely prophet and director to me. She also said this morning I must pray for a spiritual director.

I must also say she has been telling me for over a year that she felt I should be doing something scriptural. I deftly ignored her, which I tend to do with many prophets He places in my life. After Father, she was praying the next morning and God told her I needed to pray scripturally. I was praying that morning also and thought, "I really need to get some kind of prayer office." The doorbell rang shortly after and Sister handed me a daily office, along with two other prayer books. Unlike me, Sister listens when He makes a request. She responds immediately. I am learning.

Saturday

This morning I prayed the rosary in bed. Distracted, there were several things that crossed my mind that I could have been doing and I made an act of determination to stay there and finish, regardless of how badly I wanted to get up and get on with these tasks. The sorrowful mysteries limped along and I apologized to Jesus for being so cavalier about His passion. At the fifth mystery I was prompted to get out of bed and kneel down. Let me clarify. Out of my warm quilts and into the cold air of morning. I made a half-hearted attempt to ignore the prompt but it didn't go away and out I got. I was concerned regarding a friend with a problem and did not know what to do. Jesus asked me to pray the fifth sorrowful mystery for this friend. Half way through the decade He told me He would answer my prayer. I feel peace now about it, and will do whatever He asks me to do. I am confident He will direct me.

Often He is silent during my prayer of the rosary, scripture, or other structured prayer. I could say always but fear there are times when He interjects quickly, as in telling me He would answer my prayer.

On Good Friday, for example, I was in my own spiritual and personal anguish and was going to take a bath after a long, long, horrid day filled with all manner of suffering. I ran the water in the bathroom, and I heard Him calling me to kneel down and say the sorrowful mysteries. I tried to ignore Him. I mean I have to stress the dreadfulness of the day, which had been offered up for my Jesus. I went back into the bathroom and interiorly heard Him give an anguished, tortured call to me to come and comfort Him. It was from a soul, a person, a human in agony. I went back into my bedroom and knelt down and said the rosary as best I could, given my fatigue. Afterwards I went in to take a bath and He called me again. Like an overdone mother I glanced at him interiorly as if to say, "Are You kidding me?"

And He said, *"Now it is My turn to comfort you. You left too quickly."*

I went back and knelt down and We conversed about suffering and its value. Afterwards I was peaceful, trusting that He would lift my difficulties when He desired.

The point of that story is that He listens to the prayers, as He did that night. He listened to my rosary and only then did He move to speak with me. Based on my experience of God's goodness, He only wanted to comfort me, and His cry of anguish was the only way to get me back to Him to pray. Had He prompted me saying, *"I want to comfort you."* I would have said, "Forget it Jesus, it's all for You," really being just too tired and despondent to interact. I'm not expressing this well. He used His anguish to comfort me. This is what He does.

These past few days, during which I have been very sick but still functioning, which is the norm, His voice has been quiet or indistinct, causing me to question whether or not it is Him or my imagination. This is an annoyance of mine at times. This voice began in Medjugorje, where I said that my Communions were like conversations with Jesus, and that's the best way to describe it. This morning after I prayed the rosary, His voice came, but quietly, and I thought, "Is it Him or is it me?" In response to this in the past, He interrupted me and said, ***"Don't worry. I will make Myself heard."***

I laughed at this thinking that if He wanted to be heard in my house, with our five children, that is the right approach.

Anyway, this morning, I interrupted the indistinct voice and with a wave of love. I said "Jesus, I don't care if this is Your voice or not. I don't care whether I hear You or not. I know You are here, I know You have not left me, and it doesn't matter what I do as long as I serve You. So come, go, do that thing that makes Me Your best servant. I want to do one thing today. But if You prefer, I will sweep the main street of the town. Given, this would cause talk, but I am Your servant, Christ, and I know You love me. If I don't feel You close, it is only because You have momentarily let go of the bike."

Such an outpouring of love I felt, my soul was at a loss. I could not express it or the longing I felt to do what He wanted me to do. My daily grind of house-work, children, and the tantalizing possibility of some writing loomed ahead of me like a lovely thing now. I would serve Christ in my duty and that was all I needed or wanted. On I went in this vein. And the voice came back. Distinctly.

He said, *"You are learning. Do you see now what practice does for My little one? This is how a true follower responds to My love. You are learning because you are practicing. I am here. I love you. And I will never leave you. We will work together today, like every day, and you will serve Me well."*

I did not have a clear idea of what this day would bring, so I left it to Him. My intention, to sneak a couple of hours of work in past the husband, was quashed when I asked the husband if I shouldn't go and get a little work done. He said "No, leave it until Monday and start fresh." He had some wiring to do at the farm. I immediately saw the hand of Jesus and said "Fine, I'll run the house then." Jesus is pretty clear sighted on my being with the kids if they are not in school. Since our relationship became this pronounced, His timing is a marvel. Large tasks are completed on Friday often, and He makes it clear that my mothering comes first. I don't like leaving the children anymore for work, and that has been minimized with my newest projects.

Something that concerned me in reading about various saints is that they all got to a point in life where they don't want to die, but want to stay here and work for the glory of God, at terrific personal expense of course, which is the name of this game. I never felt that. I felt I wanted to be with God right away, to end the ache. I often say in times of distress, come and get me, Lord. Now. I don't want to stay here anymore.

Once, when I attended a conference, where Ivan, the Medugorje visionary, received an apparition of the Blessed Mother, I began to sob afterwards. My husband was perplexed. He felt very peaceful. I cried because she was gone and had left me. I felt bereft. Once during another crying jag I prayed to the Blessed Mother and she said, *"Wouldn't it be better to stay here and serve our Jesus?"* I was inconsolable at the time and replied like an overtired child, snapping, "No. I can't do this hard work anymore. Take me now."

Anyway, this absence of desire for God's greater glory didn't keep me up nights. I realized I was miles from these people and still am. Yesterday after Communion, as my baby disturbed my worshiping comrades, I told Jesus my concern was that He would have work for me to do, and work He wanted done, and because of my mediocrity it would not get done, or would be incomplete. This is a great fear of mine and *would* keep me up nights. He said, *"Do you see? You are learning again. You*

15

are expressing desire for My greater glory. You have it. You are coming along nicely. I am with you. You will serve Me well."

I attempted to help a friend, the one Jesus said He would take care of. I don't feel it went well. She was upset with my pointing out this small thing. I did as I felt Jesus wanted me to do, but this was not comfortable for me. Afterwards, I went to Him and said, "That didn't go well, Lord. Help me."

He said, *"You were another warning bell for her. Don't worry now. I will help her. Go on with your day."* I need to practice Holy Indifference more effectively, to keep me in the present. This is difficult, as you want to hang on to things yourself, as opposed to giving them to our Christ, who will make short work of them.

Jesus shouldered His cross willingly. The only thing that could save mankind, each person, was the cross. That part is complete. Salvation is available to every soul. Period.

But each soul must confront their sins, say I am sorry, and accept the forgiveness of Christ.

During the Stations of the Cross, I arrived at the Second Station where Jesus is given His cross. He told me this. Jesus accepted His cross with the knowledge that the mission was about to be completed. His beloved children, their precious souls, would now have the opportunity to share in eternity and arrive where they belong, with their God, who is all love. I was overcome with such a compelling feeling that none of this sacrifice be wasted. God wants every soul back with Him in our heavenly home. I prayed that God would soften the souls of every person so they would put their hand up and say "Yes, I did these bad things. I am sorry. Please bring me back to goodness." I felt this so powerfully I cannot describe it and prayed earnestly.

Jesus said, *"Do you see? You are now learning to share in My thirst for souls. You are always concerned that you don't share these holy sentiments but you are coming along. Yes, this is Our goal: that the souls of your brothers and sisters not be lost. Shoulder your cross today as willingly as I did. You note you are sick but not too sick to perform your duties. This is as I have willed. Offer your illness to Me. There will be certain days when your only duty is to accept illness. Again, it is My will. Be docile, child, and you will have the peace you desire."*

He also made clear to me that He wanted me to fulfill a certain duty, which I had been ducking with determination. I will make the call today. He also told me never to worry about my spiritual journal.

"I will see to it. It is My affair."

Praise God

During the worst of Good Friday's sufferings, I gazed at the cross. I heard in my soul, "He didn't spare His own Son. Don't expect Him to spare you." This referred to suffering, of course and gave me no manner of comfort. It confirmed that my suffering would be used and was part of something bigger, which is the salvation of souls of course.

I remember praying hard for a particular soul. This person had wronged me in many ways. I was injured yet again and complaining. Jesus conveyed to me, with as much irritation as you ever see from Him, that one day I was begging for this soul's conversion and the next I was irate because I had to offer up a little mortification. I felt His attitude was "Which is it? What do you want? The salvation of this soul? You have to be ready for a little bit of sacrifice." That probably shouldn't be in quotes as I don't remember exactly how it was worded. I'm not expressing this well because it is more my thought than His. What I'm saying is that I was given to understand at this time that there was a price tag attached to this salvation work. It was no good for me to plead with heaven and then adroitly side-step any suffering, which, of course, will be used to save such souls. I recall something being said to me like, "You have been begging us for a week, to convert this soul. Yet the minute it costs you, you back away from the work."

I hope I have made the concept clear. It is the difference, in worldly terms, of a wealthy socialite saying "Yes, feed the hungry, house the poor," but not missing even a manicure appointment. Then see Mother Theresa, spooning soup into the mouth of a hungry child. Worthy sentiments, without action, lack power.

Last night while I was questioning the method in which I hear Jesus, the Blessed Mother explained to me that this was a gift. Like any wise parent, God had given me the gift most appropriate to me. She drew my attention to the bike I had gotten for my son and explained that I would not have given a two wheeler to my three-year-old, any more than I would have given a tricycle to my eight-year-old. The gifts we are given are appropriate for our level and growth. I had to thank God for whatever He chose to send me, and not be like children who complain and envy the gifts of others. I think it was a temptation on my part to doubt the authenticity of this voice. That slows me down spiritually, as anyone can imagine. (God is not talking to you. You're nuts.)

Earlier in the day I was criticizing another mother. Jesus noted that my plans for the next day, getting a babysitter so I could work, were no better, and that I am very quick to judge others, obviously not a good thing, and need to hold myself to such high standards as well. He instructed me that I would not work today, but could write in my spiritual journal. This is another frustration for me as I would like to do this all of the time. He said I must have patience, and let things happen in His time. My duties as a mother remain my first priority and this is being drilled into me at all times. There is conflict because I am a working mother, who works from the home. Lately Jesus is structuring my time personally. I guess eventually I'll figure out that I am not to work when the children are home. For now He has to keep telling me.

One day I was praying the stations in the church. When I got to the last, where Jesus is laid in the tomb, I knelt down and prayed to the Blessed Mother. I was struggling with a decision on whether or not to speak to a group of students on spirituality. I didn't want to. I had other engagements scheduled and after taking the time off to write, felt rusty. I said, "Mother, what do I tell them?"

In my soul I saw her extend her hand to the right. I sensed she was in pain. *"Tell them this,"* she said. I looked where she indicated at the last station, where Jesus is laid in the tomb. She was saying, *"Tell them Jesus died for them."* I thought back on the death of a loved one and how horrid it was to walk away and actually leave the body. I asked her if that was hard for her.

"It was the hardest thing I ever did," she replied. I understood that she was never the same afterward. She told me that in the future, when I lost someone, to come to her there and she would console me.

This occurred a few days later. She was giving me the means to be consoled in advance.

Jesus asks us to focus on people's strengths and attributes, rather than their flaws. Shining a light on someone's good qualities is like sunshine on plants. It makes them grow. If we focus on their flaws, or negative qualities, it has the same effect in a negative way. We must practice being supportive and not critical, even in the face of the faults of others.

In prayer last night I asked Jesus if I would hear His voice or see His face while on earth. He said *"No."* This filled me with dismay. I have to say that I yearn for Him and His presence. As I said, sometimes His voice is indistinct and my need to be with Him so great that I will do a spiritual communion. He understands and is patient with me. Initially saddened by this answer, the Blessed Mother consoled me, saying that I would be near her and she would reveal herself to me when the time was right. I went to sleep with this thought. In the light of day I am thinking, what is it to me? What matter if He comes or goes while I'm on earth, as long as He is accomplishing His will in me. Earthly things continue to lose their appeal, but my work is flourishing, despite the limitations on the hours. Jesus is blessing my obedience I think.

Part of the way this gift first became apparent to me was in communions. I would begin to approach the altar to receive and the Voice would begin. This morning I struggled with children, the constant attempt to keep the house clean and the chore schedule moving forward, and the ever present hormonal challenges. It struck me that it was Sunday and I would be receiving Communion soon. This cheered me up and I was able to move more peacefully through the morning, and the throng of children undoing every job I finished.

I often compare my parenting of my children with God's parenting of us on earth. He hates us to fight. He loves us to give in and make peace, forgive, and console each other. He must get so aggravated when we fight over possessions, thinking, I gave you that and it is Mine. I can easily take it away. If you want to know how to please our God, just consider a child, and what that child would have to do to please his parents. Be good. Be nice. Be obedient. Take direction when it is given. Laugh a lot. Smile. And clean up your messes. Don't be greedy or unkind and whatever your job is, do it cheerfully.

Doing the Stations, which are rich for me, I came upon Simon of Cyrene, reluctantly helping Jesus. This breaks my heart. How dreadful to be helped grudgingly. I so often think that Jesus loves a cheerful giver. I spent a good deal of time in this hospital or that one and when a nurse was grudging or impatient in her care, it stung terribly.

As a sick person, you don't have a lot of fight or esteem, and are vulnerable to this additional wound of your emotions. At the same time I consider the great kindness and love that has been given to me in hospitals and it overwhelms me. Truly Christ is present in these loving souls. And truly nursing or any care of the sick or elderly is a blessed vocation. I think if those people who are called to those professions would ask Jesus for love, He would deluge them with graces. I ask Him right now to shower all of these souls with so much love that it pours over onto their patients and charges, badly in need of consolation.

I look at my daily duties and ask Jesus not to let me be like Simon, doing things crossly and hatefully. Of what merit is that? More dishes are clean, yes, and counters wiped, but there is no love in my kitchen. And no souls are saved or converted. We have opportunities everywhere, in every task, to salvage souls for Christ, this same Christ who took His cross in hand willingly.

On that, my children experienced a bullying situation yesterday. A small boy was assaulted, following a water fight that turned ugly. I left the house to find the culprits, filled with righteous rage. The child did not need this right now, having been victimized recently the same way. This child is also a foreigner, newly arrived in the country. And lastly, this child was in my care for the day. To make a longish story short, I found the offenders. One of my daughters and a girlfriend were attempting to exact their own justice by kicking at these boys and generally making a bad situation worse. I stormed out and lit into the boys verbally, after scolding the girls. During the tirade I mentioned that the victim had been terrorized recently. This perked their interest. I reminded them that this child was new here and in particular need of support. I threatened to go to the police. The assault had included being tossed into the lake. Now I had them frightened and a little girl who was with them watched me with round eyes. They asked who had assaulted the victim in the past and I gave a name. That's her brother, they noted. She was obviously used to dealing with the misdemeanors of her brother. The girl lowered her head in shame. This so melted me, I was speechless. "Help me, Jesus," I prayed.

I immediately changed tactics. I said that what I could not understand was that they looked like lovely boys, and I was certain that boys like them could be counted on to help strangers and play with children who needed friends. Well, the difference was palpable. One, close to tears, said, "Please, bring him back and I will apologize. I am from a foreign country and I was bullied when I got here." I said, "What on earth were you thinking?" I spoke kindly now. He said it had gotten carried away. So I agreed to go and get the boy. I said, "I knew by looking at you boys that you were gentlemen and would do the right thing." They nodded. "We will. We'll wait right up there at the top of the hill."

I went back for the victim, gave him some dry clothes, and brought him back, leaving the bloodthirsty girls behind. We stepped out of the car and the three boys approached him, carrying a bag of potato chips they had bought for him. Such genuine remorse and kindness they levied upon this boy. He was invited to play football any night the next week.

Jesus did well. He created peace where there was dissension. He made this child friends, as opposed to enemies. And He let the culprits experience their own goodness, something that surprised and warmed even themselves. I explained to my own children that night that the victim would not have wanted to face school on Monday if he was in fear. Now he had allies, instead of additional enemies.

"Jesus was bullied," I told the kids. "Yeah," said one. "They killed Him." He chose that, I explained, along with an explanation of why. Today at the Gospel we heard that Jesus lay down His life by his own choice and just as He chose to lay it down, He chose to pick it up at the Resurrection. Jesus was in charge. This made His sacrifice even more potent. He CHOSE to suffer for us. This underscored yesterday's events for the children, in that Jesus is present in every victim of every bully.

One day I took my usual walk, which winds through hills and beautiful countryside. At the highest point of the big hill, a bird flew over my head. I was struck by its grace and the effortless motion that kept it aloft. This bird was coasting on a wind. Standing alone on the hill, it was as if a veil lifted.

God allowed me to see His creation, or more accurately, how it is His creation and how it all glorifies Him and comes from Him. I could not move. I could not continue. I could do nothing but stand with my mouth open. It reminded me of St. Francis examining a flower or leaf and saying, "Stop shouting, God. I hear you." Experiences like that leave me without words. It's indiscernible. Can you say He showed me how grass grew? No. He didn't. I don't know how grass grows. It was something to do with it all fitting in together, the breeze, the sky, the animals, the sunshine and rain. It was as if I was allowed for a brief time to see the whole puzzle, all fitted together. Afterwards, I went about my business, still piecing the parts of life together, but for a moment I had viewed the end result.

"Nature is not God. I am God. Nature is a manifestation of Me as the Creator, as are all of you, My children. This is a grave error currently in the world. People are substituting nature for Me. In this instance, nature becomes no different from any other pagan god. This displeases Me."

A new health food store opened up in a nearby town. I drifted in and began to converse with the owner. He proudly showed his various departments for health and healing. He had an extensive book section. Each featured some thing or some strategy for being a whole, healthy person. It struck me though that it was ridiculous. As if each was an arrow pointing in one direction, and the next one pointed in another altogether. Conflicting arrows, advice, and ideologies, each claiming to have the answer. There was nothing there on spirituality or God or religion. I left with a heavy heart about this, but consoled myself that God is calling many to be leaders during these days, and if we cooperate, even the smallest bit, He can strategically place more and more arrows pointing up to Him, our God.

Today Jesus told me to stop swearing. This was not a request. He said, *"Stop swearing. It profanes Me. I am with you. I walk down every street with you. I go into every shop with you. When you speak, I speak with you. You must not use vile language. It brings weakness upon you, and makes it difficult for you to serve Me."*

This scolding made me feel terrible. I will make every effort to staunch the flow of bad language. It is culturally acceptable here and the habit must be starved.

I was attempting to say the Stations after Mass and there were little pockets of people chattering in the church. I couldn't concentrate. This irritated me to no end. I offered it up, thinking they should be talking to Christ here in the church. I also thought of St. Therese and how she prayed a prayer of endurance when another nun's habit of clicking her teeth disturbed her. My next thought was that I had probably been guilty of this same irritating behavior in the last week. How short are our memories when it comes to our own transgressions.

I was worried that my prayer be disturbed by my concern over what to write in the journal. The Blessed Mother said, **"Do not worry about your journal. We will tell you if you are doing something wrong."**

When I entered a strange church for the first time, I looked around, examining the architecture, etc. It would not have been my choice, and I did not love the design. I gave a sigh, and looked at the tabernacle, with the crucifix hanging above it. Oh well, I thought, it gets the job done. It immediately struck me that it was kind of like me, imperfect, guilty of flaws and not at all ideal. But Jesus was using me, in all of my imperfections, to move His plan forward. Kind of like driving an old car. You might not go fast. You might have delays. And often you might have to coax and prod. In the end, though, you usually arrive at your destination.

The more spiritual work we do, the more we practice following Christ in even the smallest details of our lives, the faster our car will drive for Jesus. I guess this is the movement to unify our will to His. We all must strive to be fast cars. What a curious analogy.

While waiting in line for Communion, I felt a deep longing or need to be infused with the Holy Spirit. I was "slain in the Spirit" once and think I would like that to happen again. I'm hoping Jesus has this planned for me as sometimes this is how that works. The desire comes, and before you know it, there you are. He sends it. Please send it to me, Lord. Perhaps it is another manifestation of my desire to be with Him. Like a child coming at the same request from a different angle, after being told no to something. (This occurred soon after.)

I want to write more but Jesus wants me to work on something else. He says I must discipline myself to stop when I'm told. How much there is to learn, and how manifold the opportunities to please Him. Of course I'm still writing, thereby talking about doing what I'm told, but not actually doing it. Okay. I've stopped.

I finished a presentation and was kneeling down before bed praying for the attendees. One woman had come up to me afterwards. I noticed her during the talk, and then, in the crush of people, she leaned in to me and made a remark about suicide. What pierced me when I had time to think about it there, praying, was the pain in her face. I nearly could not bear it. I began to beg Jesus to make that pain go away. It was such a pure, good face, the face of this woman. And it was the face of someone who had suffered. I could not even find the words to beg Jesus, except to repeat, "Please, please, Jesus."

Jesus asked me, *"What? What do you want for her?"*

I couldn't put words on it. I stammered around, repeating, "Please, please."

He said, *"You want Me to heal her. Isn't that it, My child? You want your Jesus to heal this poor soul."*

I said, "Yes," in relief. Why couldn't I find that? "Yes, Jesus, I want you to heal her. Here I am, doing your will, trying my hardest. Heal her for me."

He said, *"Are you willing to suffer for her, little one?"*

Well, everything stopped. I hate to suffer. And I am a professional sufferer, much to my dismay. My voice answered "YES," before I could put my hand over my mouth.

"Very well. I am healing her now. She is already healed."

I resisted the urge to give just a little swear and asked, "Am I going to suffer very much?" wondering of course, what I had signed on for.

"No. You are suffering now and will suffer for awhile, but I will be with you through it."

I had been working hard and travelling and for various reasons was experiencing joint pains, a headache, weakness, and general horridness. In addition, the bed in my hotel room was damp, which had left me tossing and turning the previous night and stiff the whole day. I was anticipating another night in that bed but had kept the heat on all day and aired the sheets. Additionally, at the presentation, a man had approached me and let me have it verbally. This upset me but I prayed for him and certainly understood he had a lot of problems. Well I lay down to rest, after taking two aspirins and working for another hour. I lay in bed thinking, I don't care how damp the bed is, I'm so exhausted I will have to fall asleep. Now I know better than that, but that's what I thought.

Suddenly, a fight began in the room above me. My first thought was, great, there is someone else in this scary old building. My second thought was, I hope nobody gets hurt and I don't have to call the police. I would happily do that, if someone were getting hurt. After two hours of this, I was ready to hurt them myself. The argument ebbed and flowed. The situation was close to being funny, but not quite. My joints hurt, my head hurt, my back hurt, my bed was wet, it was cold, sleep was out of the question, and I had a gruelling, taxing, 18-hour day ahead, when I would need all of my faculties.

The next morning I stared at my reflection in the mirror. A swollen face with squinty eyes took stock of me. How on earth would I work like this? He said, ***"You are right. You are powerless. Without Me, you can do nothing. But with Me, you can do anything."***

Once again, I would have to trust God to get His job done. I certainly was not capable. But this was what it took to take that look away from that woman's sweet face. God is good and I praise Him with all of my heart. This has never happened to me before. I would suffer terribly during various novenas for people, understanding that perhaps they needed a lot of grace. I will probably never see this woman again. That is fine. I picture her face, only now with peace and joy, and I love God so much.

He is very good to us.

Thoughts
on Spirituality

–2–

Thoughts on Spirituality—2

I read a piece, largely based in scripture, about the remnant and the masses. It was a good essay but I had a sad feeling. I asked Jesus, saying, "Jesus, surely You love these masses. They're all Your creatures, just like the remnant. They're not paying attention I know. But what's to happen to them?" This was His response:

"Heaven is filled with the masses. The ranks of the great saints, however, are reserved for the remnant."

Saint Faustina once saw a vision. Jesus was crucified on the cross. After a brief bit of looking at Him, she saw three groups of people. The first group were also fastened to crosses. Those were mostly religious. The second group of people were not fastened to their crosses but carried them willingly. The third group dragged their crosses along behind them, discontented, no doubt, complaining.

Certainly, we all must strive to be in that first group, willingly accepting our crosses. But I don't think that always happens overnight. Perhaps there is movement between these three levels, as a person reaches closer to perfection. So if we are not in that first group, and I know that I am not, we should not lose heart and think we are not intended for such heights. I think if we are even in that third group, where we are dragging our cross behind us, complaining all the while, we should say, "Well, I'm in the ballgame anyway. I have my cross and it's coming with me. I am a follower of Jesus Christ and that makes me a contender for greatness. Jesus will bring me along if I trust Him and perhaps one day I will shoulder my cross a little more willingly. Then, on another day, I will agree to be fastened to it for the sake of my brothers and sisters, so desperately needing grace and love."

These brothers and sisters of ours are not always easy to love, anymore than we ourselves are always lovable. We should not worry because we do not feel these sentiments. Love of souls, at least in my case, came well behind love of Christ. And love of Christ? Is there anything more natural, more instinctive, more piercing to us, His creatures? No. If you don't feel a strong love for Jesus Christ, the Man and the God, you simply don't know Him well enough. Pay closer attention during the Gospels. Read Scripture. He is there and when you hear Him talking, both to His apostles and to your soul, you will feel the overwhelming love He has for you. Think of the Ascension. *"I go to prepare a place for you. So that where I am, you also will be."* Spend some time with that line of scripture. He's saying, I'm bringing you with Me. I can't be without you, little soul of my heart.

He also repeatedly says, *"Don't be afraid. Do not fear. I am with you. I will never leave you."*

Jesus loves you. Ask Him to put love in your heart for Him. He will not refuse this prayer. Ask Him all day long until you feel it. It will come. And then you will begin to know Him. And then you will begin to love Him. Shortly after, you will begin to love your brothers and sisters and there will be no stopping the progress of your soul. You will find yourself in that first group in no time.

Someone recently asked me about uniting our sufferings to Christ. It's a bit hazy until you give it a little thought. The gift of His life, on the cross, to redeem us or ransom us back, is adequate. It is perfect. God our Father would joyfully redeem each one of us using that sacrifice alone were we willing to be saved. Not everybody is willing, though, at every moment of their lives. The pull of the world can be strong.

When we say we unite our sufferings with those of Christ, what we are doing is agreeing to be fastened to our cross. We are in that first group for that time. Well, you might ask, what's the point? Jesus did the job.

This is true. But there is a subtlety and a distinction to be made. Our suffering is not ransoming souls. That work has been completed. But our suffering is buying precious graces, graces that can be used for suffering souls, sinning souls, hardened souls, dying souls, souls in error, in ignorance, souls being victimized, abused. Souls on the brink of hell can be brought back with our sufferings. We're trading them in for graces. The Blessed Mother, the Mediatrix of All Grace, takes our little offerings and uses them to buy mercy for souls, despite the horrendous behavior of us in this modern world.

Let me put it this way. There is an alcoholic. He is steeped in sin, both with regard to this addiction and in general. Recovering alcoholics will tell you they got a tap on the shoulder at some point and their life changed. They were given the eyes to see their addiction, their selfishness, their sinfulness. They then got sober and became some of the greatest servants of Christ. Truly motivated now, these humble souls commit themselves to helping others to see. Where did the grace come from, to get them the tap on the shoulder? From our suffering, united to the passion of Jesus.

Think of Saul, getting bounced from his horse. Think of your own conversion. Did you ever sin? Were you, for a time, in the state of mortal sin? I was. Someone suffered for me, and the Blessed Mother came and collected me.

I saw a man speaking once. He was a true servant but a loud, passionate one, which sometimes alarms me. He thundered from the pulpit, shouting, "Where were you when I was steeped in sin? Where were you, when I was living the life of the world? Why didn't you come and convert me?" Well I'm looking around at the audience and most were elderly. Most were daily communicants, like myself, and I wanted to stand up and shout back, stop yelling at these people. These older souls have been praying for us, offering up their sufferings for us, and saying their rosaries for us their whole lives. In my opinion we should have been thanking this group because they were the reason he and I were converted servants of Christ. Without them, perhaps we would have persisted in our errors. They united their sufferings and prayers to Jesus.

One last thought on this. Think of Jesus' Passion as a big present. I mean the biggest you can imagine. As big as a house. It is wrapped in the most precious gold paper, with exquisite bows and garlands around it. The gift is so beautiful it takes eternity to walk around it, study it, and admire it. There are countless different facets of this gift. The study of it will indeed take your lifetime, and much longer.

Now say you want to emulate that gift. Do you have the power, the technology, the creativity to come close? Not on your best day, of course. You were not intended to create that glorious a gift. But this big gift is going to your dad, so you want to enclose some well wishes too. So you get a little gift and you wrap it up in the closest thing to the gold paper you can find. And you set your little gift at the foot of the big one. That is uniting your sufferings to Christ's. When your Father sees this gift, from His beloved child, does He say, "What a little gift. How puny it looks next to this big one."? Hardly. He smiles, like any father, and His heart is moved to all manner of generosity by your love and effort. His heart is gladdened. This is uniting your suffering to Christ.

When we all do it, there are countless little gifts around Jesus' big one. We are helping. We are doing our part. And this is certainly beneficial to the souls of our hurting brothers and sisters. But, don't forget for a moment that our God is more generous than we can imagine. He will repay us for each little gift in a spectacular fashion. It's what you might call a win/win situation. So unite your sufferings to the sufferings of Jesus in His passion. You will never be sorry. And if your suffering is the reason I was converted, I humbly thank you. And I will thank you and pray for you for all eternity, my dear comrade soul.

Jesus wants me to ask for gifts, the gifts of the Holy Spirit and the gift of healing. I began to ask, having been given the urge, but stopped myself. I am not worthy of these gifts and it frightens me. I think the words I used were, "Jesus, I don't want to get too big for my spiritual britches." Jesus responded that He is the Judge of how big my spiritual britches are to be and my urges and desires come from Him. I must be more placid and trust Him to take care of things. He will move me along as quickly as He desires and I have to let Him do that.

Yesterday I was longing for Him all day. It had been four days since I had received Communion. Far too long. My spiritual communions give me strength and sustenance and truly, all manner of comfort and guidance. He is so generous and kind to me. Well, I remembered that First Holy Communion was taking place so I scurried to organize the house so I could scoot out for thirty minutes. I timed it well and received Communion. Refreshed, I continued with my day.

Later, I was given the opportunity to take a walk. I remembered that 7:30 Mass was taking place and the desire to receive tore at me. I started to ask God if it was okay for me to go to Mass again, if it was His will, but sensed for some reason that He was going to say no so I didn't ask. It was a beautiful communion and I was able to do the stations afterwards. During prayer later that night I asked Him if this upset Him. He said. *"How could I be upset by such love? I am with you, My child, and your desire to be united to Me comes from Me. You don't always do exactly what I want but I turn things so they benefit both your soul and My plan."*

In discussing some personal matters, Jesus said, *"I respect your humanity and your vocation. Remember that both come from Me. Never worry on that accord."*

I'm in one of those funks, reminiscent of Lent. This is dreadful. I will try to describe it. Walking does not help, sitting does not help. Eating is no good. Company is torture but being alone stinks. I'm what someone might call sixes and sevens. I am seriously asking God now to send me someone to talk to. I don't want to cry because the children are not in bed. The Blessed Mother said after my afternoon rosary that I must ask Jesus for the gifts of the Holy Spirit. She reminded me to ask Him and said that He wanted to give them to me. I said, "Mother, I can't even remember for certain what they are. I'll have to go and look them up." She said I would know them when I got them.

Why this reluctance on my part? I suppose because I'm afraid of what Jesus is going to ask of me and whether or not I'll be able to do it. What if I fail? Now I know, intellectually, this is not possible because He will do for me what needs doing for me. And of course I did ask for them immediately. I don't know what is wrong. People would think I was crazy. I don't feel crazy. I am clear sighted. I think if I'm honest I'm under some kind of an attack. The devil is teasing me saying, "Who do you think you are? You think God would talk to you? What makes you think you could cooperate with a plan for Him? This is ludicrous and you should stop writing right now." Perhaps I should stop until I get a spiritual director?

God would say, ***"Did I tell you to stop?"*** He is the boss. But maybe a spiritual director would say "You are in some deep water here and should cease and desist." It might be a relief because at least I would not get it wrong.

This might be self indulgent on my part. I was talking about something today and realized I am miles away from caring about what happens with worldly things. It all means nothing. I am interested only in this work and in praying and talking to Jesus and Mary. That's for today of course. Tomorrow I'll be back working on my other project and I love that. I do love my work. All of it. I just don't want to mess this up. I think perhaps I need a hot bath and an early night. And of course, the most obvious, stick to my duty in the spirit of obedience and see what God tells me to do. I write that with the relief of a drowning man clutching a life preserver. But of course, I'll go finish my housework, put my children to bed, and pray God sends someone to sort me out. Tomorrow I'll get up and do the same. My duty is clear and I have no questions about that. So that's what I'll do. Like Lent, I'll continue on and wait for help to come. He always comes through and after these periods comes peace. But there is also the thought, "Is this the beginning of one? Or will it be short-lived?" His will be done.

Right at this time the doorbell rang and Sister arrived, bearing consolation.

During Communion this morning Jesus told me that I would not feel this way for long. Soon I will have affirmation of my duty and His will. In the mean time, I am to proceed in peace. I, myself today thought I will continue doing what I'm doing until I am told otherwise. Really, what else can I do?

During the Stations I looked at the man nailing Jesus to the cross. What kind of man is that? The only word I could think of was wretch. Take away the fact that this was God and we know that. Let's say this man did not know the victim's identity. What kind of man does that to an animal, not to mind a human being? Jesus responded that often men like this are no longer men but have given their souls over to the evil one. They are demons. But even in that level of depravity, if the soul were to stir the smallest bit, and experience a hint of remorse or guilt, Jesus would push His way in and fill that soul with Light. Such a soul does not want the Light. Jesus also said, *"I will protect you from souls such as these."*

One more thought on this. It makes sense to me because we often say that someone is a living saint, like Padre Pio, Mother Teresa, and Father Sudac. If people can be living saints, I suppose people can also be living demons. Their eternal path is secured before death. The obvious ones . . . that's not really for me to speculate.

This brings to mind the falls, during that same session of the stations. On the first fall Jesus told me again that there was no question of not getting up, despite the temptation to lay there and die, to stop suffering. He said His love for each of us was so great, He never considered anything but persevering. On the second fall He said, *"How they crowded around, to look down at Me on the ground. See the end of this Holy One? He's not so powerful now, is He? People, the bad people who allowed themselves to be led by demons, gloated and rejoiced in My falls. You have experienced this and it is difficult for you. Look at Me in My weakness, in the dirt. How your heart is moved to pity for your poor Jesus. Imagine how I feel when you fall, sometimes three times in one day. Yes, your enemies gloat, and say 'She is not as holy as she likes to think she is.' But I, I who am all light, what do I say? I say, 'She is a humble soul. Truly this soul who looks up to heaven and pleads for My help is a servant of Mine. She shall have all of the help she requires, and countless other gifts as well.' Do not worry needlessly that others disdain you. We are working together on your soul. You are coming along and I will never leave you. Peace be to you, My little one."*

This morning Jesus told me He was pleased with our meeting last night, after the family rosary. My husband closed the doors to the living room and informed everyone that we needed to talk. We created certain rules and addressed things like finding money, spending your own money without permission, no shouting, no hitting, in general a tightening up of the family behavior. It's been getting a little wild.

Jesus said, *"I want to make this family a model Christian family. This does not mean its members are perfect. It means that each is helping the others to grow closer to God. There must be love, yes, but also acceptance. I will help you. Do not worry about interference as I will protect this goal as My own. You feel embarrassed. This is because you assume the goodness will come from yourself and your humility forbids this feeling. Begin to understand that all goodness comes from Me. I will protect your humility."*

Jesus has asked me to greet the Blessed Mother after each prayer time. He does not want me walking away from a prayer time without greeting His mother as she is with Him always and intercedes for me. This morning after I prayed I said a Hail Mary. The Blessed Mother also said she was pleased with last night's family rosary. This is good because there was war before it, and war during it. We remained firm that everyone had to say it, despite the attempt of the oldest to disappear. I know that as they get older there may be resistance and it's important that we continue the rule that nobody is absent. The younger ones are watching the older ones closely to see what they can get away with. At the meeting my husband discussed their example and pointed out that the toddlers were misbehaving after watching the older children. We will have to enforce these new strategies now.

I am grateful to my husband for taking control as he did because I did not have it in me and it needed to happen. He did well and I see Jesus working in Him. I speculate that Jesus will find my husband an easy subject. He is honest, kind, and always does his duty. Thank you, Jesus, for this lovely man who is such a good father and so much fun to be around.

Anyway, during my prayer with the Blessed Mother, my mind was all over the place. She interrupted my thoughts and said, *"Go into the other room, child, if you think you can pray better there."* The other room has the big crucifix and the large statue of the Blessed Mother. That is the prayer room. I started to ignore her and continued praying and she said it again, *"Go into the other room now."* Feeling a little silly, I got up, thinking, regardless of how I feel, I have to obey. I walked out of the kitchen into the other room and saw a woman at the door outside. She was leaving something by the door. I opened the door and greeted her.

She is a friend who is very depressed. She explained that she was dropping off some small thing for me and didn't want to bother me as she knows I work in the mornings. I invited her in but she was going somewhere else. I know she feels she is imposing. I then invited her over tomorrow night with her children. This house is crazy but I knew there had to be something soon and concrete set up. She left and I went into the prayer room. It struck me that had I not gotten up I would have missed this woman. Before leaving she told me she is in "pretty bad shape." The Blessed Mother obviously did not want me to miss her. I began to pray for her and the Blessed Mother asked me if I would like Jesus to heal her. I said "yes." She asked me if I would be willing to suffer for her. Of course I said "yes," keeping both hands in front of me lest they again fly to my mouth to stop me. I understand that I am being eased into this suffering for healing exchange. The Blessed Mother then assured me that my suffering would be minimal and that I would have been suffering anyway and also explained that they are going to maximize the value of my suffering.

This makes me a little apprehensive. I don't pretend to understand how, why, or to what lengths this newest project will advance. I repeat I am trusting in Jesus to use me as He wants and I am going to repeat "Jesus, I trust in you, because frankly, I'm not thinking this would be anything I would choose." I know how that sounds but I may as well be honest. His will be done, though.

Well the suffering that day came. It lasted until 3 a.m. May God's will be done and may I always understand the value of doing His will, even when I don't understand what His will is accomplishing. It continued the next morning, which I must admit I felt was unexpected and perhaps unfair. How quickly I become disgruntled. I am truly the **accidental apostle**. I went for a rest in the afternoon and Jesus said, *"When you wake up it will be mostly finished."* He was right. I awakened and felt lighter, better, physically improved, and offered thanks that it was over.

Jesus wants firmness and follow-through with our children. I can see that many of the mistakes we make as parents are from sheer laziness in the sense that when you discipline for everything it takes energy. By discipline I mean you say, "do that." They don't, offering a muttered excuse and complaint at the unfairness of the request. Well then you must enter into the fray and force compliance. Unless of course they make a reasonable and fair argument about why your request is wrong. But the times where the parent is mistaken are few, I would think.

So there you are, forcing the child to do what he or she is told. It's easier to sigh and do it yourself or walk away and busy yourself with something else, forgetting that your child just learned that he or she is making the rules in the family. It takes energy. I repeat this because many of us parents today find we are depleted of energy. Jesus would say this is because we are squandering energy on the wrong things. We are spending our parental energy on things that are not parental.

"Parents are far too concerned with their own entertainment. The formation of their children suffers."

Obviously children need to become our priority again. And not their material concerns. Many children today are drowning in material wealth and starving for spiritual food and love. They need walks, talks, and to be listened to. These activities are free and do not require a parent to work additional hours to finance.

Lord, help us to become better parents and to give our children faith. Lord, You better help us to reacquire our faith, so that we have something to share with these children. Protect us from the distraction of the New Age and its empty promises. Bring us back, Jesus, to the path that leads to You. Bring us back to goodness, God. Draw the scales from our eyes so we can see again and, one by one, set the example that God is with us. Help us to reject this present world, with its darkness and spiritual starvation. Send us vocations, Lord. Send us brave souls, willing to push back the badness. We love You, we trust You, we rely on You, Lord Jesus Christ, our dear Savior.

Today after writing I sat with my arms crossed. I felt Jesus glance and He asked me if I weren't glad I wrote for Him today. I did not want to. Nine times out of ten I feel I have nothing to say. Jesus responds, *"That is good. You will listen to Me. I have much to say."*

Anyway, today as I sat there I said, "Jesus, I feel like a big know-it-all." He laughed and said, *"My dear child, do you really still think this comes from you? Don't you realize that you know nothing without Me? Don't be afraid. I often use people to speak through. I will protect you and I will protect My work. Now be happy because your Jesus is pleased with you."*

How can anyone not love Him? Again, the only explanation is that they do not know Him. Maybe this work will change to be all about Jesus and I can call it Jesus Exposed. Then the world will fall in love with Him and there will be no sin, no rage, no hurt and no exploiting of children. What a dream! Please God, make it happen. I want it so badly.

Jesus just said, *"You are learning again, My little apostle."*

I think the operative word there is "little."

This morning I was given to understand that Jesus was disappointed in me yesterday. At the morning's prayer He told me that He would speak with me later in the day and that I would write in the journal. The day was challenging and hectic, and by the end of it, I felt unwell and exhausted. I did not pray again until just before I was falling asleep. This morning at Communion I felt such joy and thanksgiving. Truly I overflowed with this and praised God, praised God. Jesus said that when I don't come to Him, He cannot give me graces He has planned for me. Some of these graces may be destined for others and because I don't "collect" them, they don't get delivered. This is my interpretation, of course, but it did make me see the importance. What I should have done was knelt down before Him, regardless of how briefly, and said, "God, I'm wrecked. This day has been deadly. Anything important going on? Anything You want me to do?" I am learning. I will try not to make that mistake again. I don't feel too badly, as I sometimes do, because I know I did my best yesterday, despite this small neglect. I notice though that I was quite impatient by the time I put the kids into bed and had I spent time with Jesus, however briefly, I would have done better.

During the Stations I stopped at the third fall, which goes right through me like an arrow to my heart. I said, "Jesus, how I would love to sweep You up into my arms and run with You." He said *"Today you will be given the opportunity to pick someone up who has fallen. I will tell you when it is happening. It will be the same*

as if you are picking Me up after My fall."
I imagine sweet Jesus actually hitting the hard ground, in His beaten and exhausted, weak, thirsty state. It makes me wince, with the cross probably falling on top of him. Then I shoot dirty looks at Simon, reminding myself to be a cheerful giver and helper. How well I determine the faults of others. I'm really gifted in this way. I should perhaps stand on the street and point them out to people as they pass. Jesus says, *"My child, do not judge Simon so harshly. I do want you to give cheerfully. I do not want you to judge situations or others, particularly when you do not understand the facts."* Heaven help me not to be judgmental.

Today I hope to collect any graces available to me. I have been informed that I need to suffer for someone. This will be difficult I fear, as this person is troubled to a great extent, and in some ways dangerous. Jesus told me that my suffering would not be severe. When asked to suffer for this person I said "yes." The hands flying up to my mouth are no longer a problem. I'm finally understanding that these souls are precious to my Jesus, and as such, must be precious to me. Jesus has given me a tender love for them, which makes me teary-eyed thinking of it. I find it notable that even those who have hurt me, I can feel passionate affection for, and the need to help in anyway to secure their healing and peace, and most assuredly, their poor suffering souls. Some are a joy to help. With others, the experience can be quite bitter. I have to get where I say, "What's the difference? It's all the same to me. A day in the service of Jesus is a day in the service of Jesus." To finish the point, though, in response to my question on whether or not the suffering would be severe, Jesus said, *"No. You won't suffer any more than you have been predestined to suffer."* So there you are. It's coming anyway. May as well make it count.

I often look at the picture of Little Audrey Santos on my dresser and when I've wanted to ask for her help, I've stopped myself, fearful that I would add to her sufferings. I don't remember who, but somebody on heaven's side of the fence told me that she WANTS to suffer for us and that a tiny bit of her suffering buys huge amounts of heavenly graces. So I was wrong not to ask her intercession. In other words, Audrey has terrific graces at her disposal. She wants to share them with us. Perhaps I will ask her help with this current soul, who will be a tough nut to crack I would think. That's what I'll do. I'm networking.

Jesus is asking me to see to my children so I must stop.

The suffering continues. I knew this soul would be difficult. I am unwell. This morning at Mass I felt so weak and sick. I prayed to Jesus to help me in the sense that I could not complete my duties.

He said, *"I will give you the use of My body today so that you may run your household. Your suffering is temporary. We are making good use of it, my child, so persevere."*

I must say, despite my being unwell, I am flying through my chores, chores I was certain I lacked the strength to do. He also said, *"I am with you. I have every consideration for you during your suffering. Do you see how tenderly you walk through My Stations of the Cross? I am that way with you. Such solicitude is offered to you, if you will just accept these spiritual gifts. Move slowly, child, and methodically, conserving your strength, and all will be well. I have special spiritual chores for you today. Do not groan under the weight of the cross today, as I will lighten it soon and you will only be glad you cooperated. I am with you. I will remain with you. And you will soon belong completely to Me."*

Yesterday the homily was about the rosary. The priest did a beautiful job of encouraging families to begin this prayer anew. He advocated starting with one decade. I was disappointed that my husband did not hear it because the priest also called upon the fathers to lead their families in this way.

It occurred to me though, that my husband did not need to hear it. Recently my eldest, who is balking at family prayer, said, "Mom makes us say the rosary." My husband interrupted her and said. "That's not true. I am the one making us say the rosary. It is my decision that we say it so don't think it's Mom's." He said this so firmly, with such conviction, that my daughter actually remained silent, understanding that this was not a joking matter. I, of course, was delighted as I don't like the role of the spiritual heavy. I find this changing gradually and am glad to see it of course. God is good to us.

The other day I went about my business. During the afternoon there was a great war between two of the children. Another became involved, and the original culprit was eventually sent to her room. Time passed and I offered forgiveness but she rejected it. Finally she came down, still separated from all, but agreeable to eating her dinner. She was then accidentally hit in the face, resulting in a nose bleed. Jesus said, *"She is the soul you are to pick up in your arms. Treat her as you would treat Me, fallen, during My Way of the Cross."* I was surprised as I had never considered it would be a child who would need such love and caring. I did treat her just that way and she began to sob. Truly this little child was feeling deeply all that occurred, and I did not realize how separated she felt from the family on this day.

Jesus is good to me, giving me such particular guidance. He offers this to every soul who is interested. I cannot stress this enough. He is within every soul. If a soul would take the time to converse with Jesus, Jesus would guide that soul personally, with love and wisdom. How sublime is the relationship with our Christ.

That said, I do not want people to think it is something mysterious and beyond the reach of each simple soul. It is instinctive, within us. The call to our God comes from our center, and when we are in pain, it becomes louder and more insistent. Instead of answering the call and dropping to their knees saying, "God, God, make haste to help me," people go to health food stores, fortune tellers, Reiki practitioners, and all manner of holders of empty promises. The anguish, the groaning, is the soul, saying, "Please, dear person, I am starving. Feed me with spiritual food that I may begin to flourish again, thereby granting you the peace you find so elusive." This was not always a problem, but it is a problem today. Jesus has graces but nobody is collecting them. Hmm. More for me?

That was a joke but Jesus answered, *"Yes. Exactly. An abundance of graces awaits any soul wanting them. My mother offers them to her children with such hope and tenderness. You must make this known to souls, particularly those souls who are in pain and feel unloved and forgotten.*

Such souls often accept My graces willingly. Go out and speak the name of Jesus Christ. Go out and preach the gospel. Make My name known to all, that all may be loved and be saved. I am asking this of you today, and if you look for the answer, the answer will come to you. Look closely into your daily life. Where can you evangelize? Where am I asking you to evangelize? You will be given the answer in your heart, dear one. I will put it there. Truly, you will overflow with these answers, if only you will heed the sound of My voice."

Of course, I pray, "Jesus, let us heed the sound of Your voice. Make it loud, Lord, so we cannot ignore it and go about our business. We want to serve You, Jesus, more than anything. Our love for You is small though, and blows away with worldly breezes. Make us stronger, Lord. Make us firm. Make us immovable in Your service. Bring us to those souls who are unloved and forgotten. Please, Jesus, as our Friend, we call upon You to show us Your will, and then tell us Your will clearly, so we walk with confidence on the path of heavenly service. Truly we want this Jesus, despite our fearful hearts. Give us great courage, and then more courage besides, so we will not falter and cower in the face of our duty. Lord, we want this. We are asking this of You. Please, Jesus, in the name of our Blessed Mother Mary, grant these requests. Amen."

Thoughts
on Spirituality

–3–

Thoughts on Spirituality

I was praying to the Blessed Mother tonight and told her again of my fears and feelings that I might not get things right. She said, *"We are protecting you more than you realize, my child. What little suffering We are allowing is for the good of your humility. Do not fear. I am with you."*

Jesus said again, *"See how willingly I accept this cross? If My children, even just My chosen ones, would accept their small crosses and say, 'I accept this cross in the name of Jesus Christ for the salvation of sinners,' I could save countless souls. Countless. The value of even a small thing offered to God is inestimable. You must understand that suffering will occur in every life. Use it for your holiness and for the good of your brothers and sisters."*

I stopped again at the nailing of the cross. I keep studying this man who is nailing Jesus to the cross. Jesus said, *"It would have been better for him to have refused and not participated in this abomination. He should have allowed himself to be victimized in this way before committing this atrocity. You must never fear man. Man can hurt your body but of what worth is your human body? You will relinquish it to Me in the blink of an eye. Only your soul is of eternal*

63

value. Talk about the directing of the body by the soul. This consoles Me."

I recently spoke to a group of high school students and spent a great deal of time discussing their dominion over their body. I explained that their soul and their intellect, guided by their soul, made every decision about what their body did. For example, they decided what food to put in their bodies, what to do with their hands and feet during sports, during play, during work. I asked them to remember that they had control in their sexuality especially. They must be careful, I warned, not to think for a moment that their body was making the decisions. I also warned that every "body" made suggestions to the intellect and soul about things that were wrong. These decisions, based on cravings or urges, could be wrong. It is up to the soul and intellect to say "no" to the body when the body makes a request that is inappropriate for the person. I often say to these young people that if it were true that they couldn't help themselves and were carried away with these bodily urges, then we would all need to be locked up because that is what happens to people who do not control bad desires and urges. They are not fit for society. Obviously I say this in a pleasant way, if you can imagine that. Actually, I make it quite absurd and funny.

"If a soul will trust Me, there is no limit to what I can do through her."

I must continue to work on trust. Perhaps the Divine Mercy Chaplet will help.

I prayed at the Third Station and Jesus told me that soon I would fall and He would be there for me, as I was here for Him. I was thinking of big falls, and not really equating falls with failures on my part, but thinking in terms of persecutions, attacks, crosses. We were driving in the car with the children and I won't try to describe the chaos. I will spare my reader in the interest of peace. After many futile attempts to get some kind of reasonable behavior from them, I lost my temper and swore at them. This resulted in a heavy silence. My husband said nothing. I immediately said "I'm sorry. You're making me crazy." My loyal husband replied, "They would make anyone swear." He had also had it and he was trying to drive. Anyway, I sat feeling terrible and Jesus came to me and consoled me. He made me feel immediately better, I knew I was forgiven, and felt the loveliest peace, despite the not-so-peaceful circumstances. He indicated to me that this was the fall He had been referring to. He is good to me and is never outdone in generosity.

Today started out as a difficult day. Everyone is sick, including me. Sleep last night was disrupted and uncomfortable. The day started contentiously, with disagreements over all manner of topics. Yuk. I went out to Mass alone, a rushed, stolen affair, and felt better. I was instructed to smile and be pleasant, regardless of what transpired. I have to say here that during the Mass, indeed during the first few minutes in the church, smiling became an easy thing. Once I am in the presence of Jesus, I can smile, despite difficulties.

During the Stations, which I dashed through after Mass upon request, I stopped at Jesus meeting His mother and prayed to our mother. She supported my decision to keep the children home, despite the discord this caused.

She said, *"You must trust your judgment. You made the right decision. In the future, do so calmly, and never be afraid when you are challenged if the issue has to do with the welfare of your children. But remain calm. Your peaceful firmness will say much more than becoming upset because you are questioned."*

When Jesus meets the women, I prayed for all battered women.

I can't describe my loneliness for God. I want to be with Him. I am almost tearful all day. I did two more spiritual communions and feel sometimes I am bothering the Blessed Mother, as I always ask for her intercession for these communions. During one, Jesus assured me that He was with me, and would remain with me. I asked Him what He did all day, while I was working through my duties.

He said, *"I am standing by, so that if you need Me, I am here."*

This made me smile and indeed lightened my heart considerably. Later, I was lonely again, and could not remember what He had said that I found so consoling. This caused me to nearly become tearful again. It is that kind of a longing day. So I annoyed my Blessed Mother again and said bring Him back to me. I heard his voice immediately.

He said, *"I am here. I said that I was standing by, in case you needed Me. Just like right now."*

I smile just thinking of it. I asked Him if I could come and write it down as I feel it was so lovely. I also said, "Jesus, I don't understand. How can you be in everyone in this way." He told me to think of His relationship and mine as something unique. It is nowhere else. I don't have the understanding to grasp it of course and that does not matter. It was the feeling He conveyed of love.

To think that this is available to everyone . . . people would all feel this way if they would turn to Him. I can't live without Him. I am lonely for Him quite a bit. I cannot imagine heaven because I feel such joy here. What must heaven be like?

My sister told me something once that responds to my question to Christ, asking Him how He can be with everyone. A priest once said that if a mirror broke into a thousand pieces, each piece, despite its smaller size, would still reflect. The priest used this analogy in reference to the Eucharist. Each Host in each tabernacle in all of the world is as powerful as the next, or as the first. I think this works also as to the childlike logistical question of how He can be everywhere. Silly, what the mind fixates on. It's just that when you love someone you think of all of these silly little items because when you are not with them, you think about them in all manner of ways. I know Jesus is with me. I know it on many levels. But it is not a full joining, and therefore there is the pain of longing and the anguish of being apart, although I have the joy of speaking with Him now. That is huge and I shake my head in despair of describing that joy, but I want more and more and more. Back to cleaning the bedrooms.

Before Communion I prayed to God. I have been dutifully asking God to send me His gifts, the gifts of the Holy Spirit. Next Sunday is Pentecost Sunday, which is perhaps the reason for all of this focus on the gifts of the Holy Spirit. I turned all of this around in my head as I prayed and I began to get myself confused. Finally, I prayed, "God, send me whatever gifts you choose to send me. My only prayer to You is that I not interfere with Your will because of my flaws. Beyond that, I don't care what You do, so long as I am serving You."

It can get confusing because you don't want to err in humility or desire great lofty gifts. On the other hand, you don't want to have a weak will and cloak it in false humility. I am not worthy, therefore keep your gifts so it doesn't cost me anything. There is also such a thing as thinking too much about it all, as though it were up to you and as though it were dependent on your own will. That's where I was tumbling around when I finally said, "Enough. I don't care what happens and I leave it all to you."

He responded, *"Your prayer pleases Me. It is the evidence that you are ready for the gifts I intend to bestow on you."*

Before, during and after Communion, there was a great deal of interaction about all of this. I don't feel comfortable writing about it because I fear it makes me sound as though I think I deserve these graces. I don't. I am patiently aware of my weaknesses and continued struggles. The conversations are about me accepting God's will in me, and being ready to make the sacrifices these graces will entail. I don't know what they are. I have no idea what this all means. I assume it is a deepening of Our union. I have asked for this and at one point responded to Him this morning that I don't mind what He sends as long as I can draw closer to Him. He said that Our union would be deepened as a result of Our work together.

During the First Station, Jesus is condemned to death. He said, *"You will also be condemned. You will be condemned to live in this world but not be a part of it. That is what My will for you entails."* I said, "I don't care," as I had been saying all morning. "Let my will be Your will, God."

At the Second Station, Jesus accepted His cross willingly. He said, *"Do you accept this cross willingly?"* I again replied, "Yes. I don't care, Jesus, as long as I please You. I have no fear of it as it comes from You."

He replied, *"It will come from Me. I will place it in your hands, as this cross was placed in My hands."*

By this time now I've been repeating myself all morning, I felt, saying "Yes, yes, yes." I felt like Peter when He kept asking, *"Do you love Me?"* You're kind of like, aren't You listening? Am I being interfered with here? But then you understand that this is very important and He is making a point. God knows your answers. So it must be that He wants you to hear yourself saying, yes. It must be an act of your will and because human beings are so flawed and weak willed, we have to repeat it to get used to the idea. I'm not sure of that. I'm guessing.

On to the Third Station, Jesus falls for the first time. He tells me, *"You will fall. And people will ridicule you. See them standing around Me? This will happen to you, too, but I will be there."* Again, I say, "Yes, I understand Jesus. I will hate it but I will offer it to You and You will be there to console me and pick me up."

On to the Fourth Station and Jesus meets His mother. He tells me that it might appear in the world that Jesus meeting His mother was painful. And there was pain. But Mary knew she had to be there for this reason. Jesus appeared to the world to be walking up Calvary alone. In reality, He was not alone.

His mother was present, representing all the heavenly court. They were actually there, with Mary, and when she offered this union of herself to Christ in His passion, she offered it from them all. When He looked into her anguished face He drew courage and the strength to continue. She did this for Him and this was part of her sacrifice. He drew courage from her.

Secondly, there were good and holy souls who accompanied Him. He told me that my soul, along with countless other little souls, accompanied Him to Calvary. He drew strength from us and from our presence in His passion. We consoled Him. It's some sort of backwards in time sort of thing and we cannot understand it from our position on earth. At least I am struggling with it in a logistical sense. We were with Him. We flocked around Him in a great multitude and stayed with Him until the end. He said, *"Can you see why I persevered? The love that surrounded me? This love surrounds you and all just souls."*

When Veronica wiped His face, she stood in for all the just souls on earth at the time. They were all represented in her as she held out the cloth to comfort her savior. He drew resolve from this, which made it easier to rise from His next fall.

I'm jumping around here but when Simon helped Jesus, what Jesus needed was love. Simon did not offer this. The cheerful giver offers love and makes the soul feel united in His cross. The mean, resentful giver would do better to stay away sometimes.

At the meeting of the women of Jerusalem Jesus said that women and children suffer greatly in this world at the hands of unscrupulous men. These are grave sins and God will not suffer this much longer. He looked out at them and saw innocent children and women from every time and He felt pain, and tenderness, and every bit of compassion that has ever been in the world. It is always His will to help such as these. Always.

Jesus falls the third time, and tells me that when I fall, there are souls helping me. He told me that while I pray, while I attempt to do His will in the world, and during this, my time of formation, there are countless souls in heaven who are pulling for me and helping me. He said that like Him carrying the cross with all of this 'invisible' help, I am the recipient of the same. Anyone who agrees to carry their cross and share in His passion and in His will have this, a cohort and honor guard of heavenly saints and angels who assist us and watch out for us. We are never alone.

We must look at Mary and draw courage from her as well, knowing that our Mother's face represents all the heavenly court and that is what is at our disposal. Jesus also sends people into our lives like Veronica, who is basically His representative on earth and who is sent from Him. This person represents all of the servants on earth right now, who wish us well and whose prayers and sacrifices can be and are being used to help us when we need graces. He is trying to convey the grandeur, the majesty, the bigness of our team or side. We should never be afraid. The other side, the side of darkness, is not organized, supportive, or consistent. There is no question of which side will triumph. It is a non-issue. The only issue is that we push back hard at the wave of badness so souls will see their errors and find the peace that is Christ. A big hard push is necessary right now.

As Jesus is stripped of His garments, today I hate it, as usual, this final slap and humiliation for our Christ. But I see it as something else today. It was a nothing in heavenly eyes. Worldly humiliation is a nothing. We should yawn in the face of it because it is so fleeting and who are we being humiliated in front of? Good and holy souls do not exult in this. Our heavenly friends see it as nothing. So we fear the disdain of worldly souls? If this is so, we need to target that as an area of spiritual work.

I remember once worrying about something years ago. I don't remember what it was. But it definitely had to do with what others would think of me. Jesus said to me, *"Try to impress Us, your heavenly friends."* Well I walked on air for days. Every time I thought of it I laughed. He was telling me to impress the saints with my fortitude, my patience, my humility, my making myself small and serving others. It helped me, it really did, to see things differently. It is a good approach to our spirituality and to the walk with Christ. We should treat worldly applause and approval as nothing except a possible danger if we become attached to it, and treat heavenly approval as our primary goal.

I am a little concerned regarding Jesus having this assistance or consolation during His Passion because I have always been taught that He felt abandoned. He tells me not to fear. He felt abandoned by God and the union with His father that He was accustomed to had been separated during this, His time of Passion. He was meant to feel abandoned by God. But that did not mean souls could not comfort Him and did not comfort Him. This is how we sometimes feel, on a lesser scale, when He lets go of the bike or we are in a period of aridity. We must always remember that God is there, despite our feelings of aloneness. I have a plaque that says, Bidden or Unbidden, God is present. Padre Pio said, *"Aridity is the fruit of our defects."* Well said, although it took me years to understand it.

On the First Station today, Jesus pointed out that when He received the death sentence and was condemned to die, He felt a momentary feeling of panic and revulsion. It was His humanity protesting at the idea of its death. He said we need to separate ourselves from the world and practice detachment from worldly things, human respect, and at times even people. We must separate because if we become too attached to these things, we cannot serve Him with completeness, which is what we are striving to obtain, completeness in Christ and in service to Christ. That is our goal, and we must set our spiritual bar very high. If we practice this, and make it a habit, we will not be disappointed or drown under the inevitable situation where the world or its people withdraw their esteem or affection from us. At times, if you are in the service of Christ, you will be attacked. When your eyes are set on heavenly things and you are detached, you will suffer the initial feeling of revulsion at this, and perhaps panic, but soon your focus will realign itself, your will will make the correction, and the attack will not disturb your peace too much. I think the great saints remained recollected in times of attack. They abhorred too much affection and ran from adulation. They knew.

Something my Blessed Mother wants written is this. Upon consideration of the third fall this morning, I was struck by the divinity of Christ. There He is, laying in the dirt, and He still has the halo of light surrounding His head. This must show us that Jesus was divine during all of this. The point He wants to make with us is this. The world could not accept Him because of the way He came, as a humble carpenter's son. The world, or the foolish in the world, despised His lowliness. We cannot do that.

She says, *"You must look for the road to heaven in the small, lowly things. Your service to unloved or forsaken people, who cannot repay you, either with esteem, money, or even admiration, is what melts the heart of your Jesus and impresses your heavenly friends. The unseen service is to be desired."*

Today I hurried through the Stations as people were waiting for me. I sometimes feel I need to be five people. I was half-praying and half-saying, Jesus, I have to go. Jesus said at the Fifth Station, *"You may go. I will be with you."* I felt a little bad but not too badly as these are not play things I had to do. An ailing father-in-law needed to be driven to the doctor, my daughters were waiting, nobody is getting enough attention from me it seems and I am pulled in pieces. Anyway, He reminded me to, *"Greet My mother."*

I said a Hail Mary and she let me have it, saying, in summary, **"You long for my Son and miss Him when you feel you are far away. Now, during this, the time you have set aside for Him, you hurry out. There are precious things that He wishes to teach you, and to teach others."**

Well, you can imagine how I felt. Obviously I finished the Stations. The above paragraph, which I'm not sure I did justice to, was what the Blessed Mother did not want forgotten or unclaimed. I dash off again, feeling I've given this short shrift but being pressured to hurry up for these last ten minutes. Christ be praised.

Along the lines of that last thought, feeling overwhelmed, I continue. I had a very difficult weekend with the children. Sunday deteriorated to shouting and yelling, really on the part of everyone, and I felt this as a painful failure. I tried praying and asked Jesus for patience but soon after exploded and joined the children in the shouting, accusing game. I think I won, in the short term. They cleaned up their messes and went to bed quietly. On the other hand, I felt such shame and remorse. I know Jesus does not want this. He wants calm and firmness. But honestly, a couple of them are in bad phases and would try the patience of Job. Regardless. That is not the point. Children are challenging and to set an example of shouting and losing one's temper results in exactly those behaviors in these children. I know that. I felt very badly and was so discouraged and disheartened I barely prayed at all. I avoided God.

The mood stuck this morning as I made my way to Mass with the baby. She was noisy and disobedient and I barely communicated. I did say, "God, you have the wrong lady here. I'm falling apart at the seams. I'm swearing. I think I told one of the children that I hated her yesterday. Leave me to drift off. I can't do this feeling so weak and unwell." This is what happens to me. I lose it.

My tone was not accusatory, although I did feel a little let down as I asked for help during the fray and lost it anyway.

When I brought this to His attention He said, *"I cannot get in front of you and your free will. Next time, go into another room and give Me a moment to place peace in your heart."* Okay. That sounds reasonable.

Regarding my general feeling of handing in my notice, He said, *"You are quick to become discouraged. You are not a saint. You will experience your weakness. To despair over your weakness is a failure in humility. Expect to fail. Expect to need My intervention and sustaining hand. Do not be surprised when you feel the sting of your humanity. It is part of your cross, My child, to be so close to Me and remain so imperfect. Be at peace. Am I threatening to leave you? Is My mother threatening to abandon you? It will never happen. I will repair the damage to your little family and help you and your husband to guide your children through these difficult days. You must continue to serve Me, as I need you. We must write for souls, My dear one. I have forgiven you. Have you forgiven yourself? Onward. Always onward. I have prepared many graces for you and you must continue to collect them. You are like a butterfly with a sore wing and you fly with great effort right now. It will not always be this way. Soon you will soar and not feel the effort. This will happen through My intervention. You noted recently that you did not have to worry about obtaining the gifts of the Holy Spirit. You were quite correct. It is up to Me. It is all up to Me, My spiritual infant. You can rest easily, knowing Jesus will bring you along as quickly as He needs to, so that you can serve Me in the capacity I have chosen for you. Be at peace. I will never leave you."*

There is not much for me to add to that, as I am so moved and consoled. How good He is to us, and how patient.

Thoughts
on Spirituality

–4–

Thoughts on Spirituality

"I want to speak directly to souls at this time. Many souls are crying out for Me. They think I do not hear. It is they who do not hear. They are not listening for My voice, which must be heard in the silence of their heart. A soul who does not put their self in a quiet state will not hear Me. You, My child, have just blocked off your ears and closed your eyes for ten minutes in order to focus wholly on Me. And We are communicating in a supernatural way. But you understand that in order to hear Me, and it has always been this way for you, you must block out the noisy distractions of this world, which grow louder by the day."

"I would encourage souls to remove noise from their lives. Turn off the televisions. Turn off the radios. Many conversations are better avoided. In this new silence they will find their heart recollected. In their recollected heart they will find Me, who has been waiting for them."

"I am here, dear soul. You need only look into your heart. I ache for you, for your pain, for your loneliness, for your isolation. Each soul feels alone at times and understands that human consolation is

empty. They must seek spiritual or heavenly consolation. If you feel a stirring inside, it is your soul, seeking Me. Answer your soul, My dear lost one, for you will find Me waiting and I will solve all of your problems. I can work in you in miraculous ways if only you will allow Me. You have sought other consolations, which have disappointed you. Now try Me. I am here. I love you. I await you."

"I want to address holy souls. So often you become discouraged. You do not bear with yourself at all. I, your Jesus, have endless patience with your flaws and weaknesses. You must trust Me to forgive you and overlook these human frailties. I am not like a spy, waiting to catch you at bad behavior. Rather, I am your friend. Your greatest advocate. I applaud your small attempts at holiness. Along with the Communion of Saints, I am pulling for you, My holy chosen souls. There is great work to be done. So let Us not waste time worrying over Our humanity. I don't expect perfection. Please do not expect it from yourself and you won't be discouraged. You must walk with confidence toward Me, always seeking My will. In the smallest details of your day, seek My will. I will make it known to you and gradually, you will live in a world that is saying "yes" to God. Hunger

will disappear, the blackness of sin will recede, and little by little, My goodness will spread to all mankind. This is not impossible. You are skeptical because you live in a world poisoned by skepticism. This skepticism does not come from Me. Be instead, filled with hope. And certainty. Be certain that the impossible is easy for Me. I could exert My divinity in this world, but I don't want to do that. I want you, My chosen ones, to bring about this Renewal. That is your mission. Impossible you say? It is not impossible for Me if you allow Me to work through each one of You. And you will be part of the greatest Renewal in the history of your world. It is coming. So be of good cheer and do not become discouraged. When you feel hopeless, come to Me, and I will infuse you with fresh hope and joy. Your work is important to Me."

The Blessed Mother says, "I am here, child. Be at peace. You do not hear Us as distinctly as you would like because you are not praying enough. You must pray more and Jesus and I can take over your life to a greater degree. I know you wish this. The trip on Sunday is my gift for you so have no fear. I want you to go. I will arrange every detail. I do this often for the little souls under my care. And I long to place every little soul under my protection. If only they would come to me."

"Jesus requires great things of His chosen souls. And any soul reading this must understand that We are talking to you. There is great work to be done. Sin, hunger, want, and destruction are the result of many, many souls refusing to serve my Son. If even one soul makes a decision to serve Jesus in a consistent way, the world begins to change. You don't see it, but it is happening. Jesus seeks a worldwide renewal. You must participate for it to be complete. You must leave the smallness of your humanity for a moment and see the world from the heavenly perspective. We, the Communion of Saints, are doing our part from heaven. We are working in the world in a supernatural way, along with countless angels. The help available to souls during this time is unlimited. Do you want to serve Christ? Do you want to be a part of this renewal? Say yes to my Son in the silence of your heart and you will see Him begin to work within you in an extraordinary way. He will build your trust and faith until you seek only His will. Your joy will overflow, little child, because you will have a foretaste of the joy of heaven, and the beautiful existence that awaits you. Do not be afraid. I am with each of you and desire to lead you along this path. You will not be disappointed if you come to us. Let nothing stand in the way of your conversion to silence. It is there you will find Jesus."

Jesus: *"I am with you, child. I feel your weakness and sickness and will adjust your responsibilities accordingly. This will pass. Offer your suffering to Me so that I can nourish souls, especially souls who are in error and in danger of falling away. My heart aches for them. They feel they have been abandoned, yet it is they who have abandoned the true faith. Suffer willingly for them, little one. We must draw them back with goodness and joy. A true follower of Mine is joyful and serene. When you see Christians who claim to be following Me, but they are sad and morose, you should be alert. Despair and depression do not come from Me. My followers are given hope and a lightness of spirit, despite difficulties. If you, yourself, notice you are feeling sad more often, it is because you are not connected to Me through prayer and the sacraments. Be vigilant about your faith and you will not falter. I am with you. I will never leave you. Ask Me for courage and courage will be yours."*

Our mother says, *"You cannot always attend Mass when you would like. This is a cross and you can offer it to Jesus. You will benefit as though you had attended, particularly on days like today when your intention to assist was present. Your decision to see to the children was correct. We are with you as you perform your duties and your duties become a prayer, particularly when you unite them to us. Remember that your vocation as a wife and mother is divine and will be blessed accordingly. Be happy, little child. You serve your Jesus well, despite your fatigue."*

Jesus: *"You will overflow with answers."*

I feel such gratitude today. On the human side, I'm grateful I have been given a few hours to rest. On the spiritual side, I was afraid I could not serve Jesus as I am so unwell, but I see that all I have to do is sit here and He sends the words. I want so badly to work for Jesus. Yesterday I sat down to do some money-earning office work and He stopped me.

"Work for Me first. Always see to My interests first. I will then bless your other endeavors."

I obeyed and felt badly that He had to tell me that. I feel I am getting better at paying attention but heaven knows just as I say that I am probably preparing for a big failing. I must get better at relying wholly on Jesus and Mary, and then I will move more quickly through His work. They are forced to go slowly with me because of my flaws.

I am off to Knock today, on my mini-pilgrimage. My son said last night, "I want to go to Knock. I think this should be a family pilgrimage." I nearly burst out laughing. No way. This little one is not interested in the prayer end of things, I don't think. He just wanted the trip. I thank God and the Blessed Mother for this day.

Jesus: *"Again you feel the weight of My cross. Unite your sufferings to Me, child, that I may benefit souls. Father is My servant. You may trust his guidance. I will leave nothing to chance and you should stop questioning My plan, method, or goals. All you need do is be at peace and do the work I ask you to do. I will never leave you. And you will never fail Me in this regard, because it is My work. Be an example of peace to your brothers and sisters so that they, too, may desire union with Me. That is the challenge to My followers. If you have a peaceful countenance, you reflect Me, your savior. Others see this and desire it. 'What is it about that person?' they ask. If you are a follower, your holiness will shine from within you and that is what they will identify. Be at peace. Fear is not from Me and does not draw you closer to Me. You must strive for confidence in your God. I will be with you, even until the end of time. Your sufferings will console you greatly later, when you join Me. You will never be sorry you suffered for your Jesus. I am bringing you along and soon you will no longer feel the weight of this cross."*

The Blessed Mother: *"The gifts I gave you in Knock will soon become apparent to you. What happiness you will experience through your charity, love of neighbor, and devotion to me. Try not to worry over this work, dear one. As Jesus said, it is His work and as such will be completed with very little effort on your part. You see that now, don't you? Some days will be more difficult than others but that is always the way. Even for me, during my time on earth, it was that way. Souls are saved through our obedient children; regardless of the difficulty they are experiencing. Please don't think that because you are struggling, your offering is less. On the contrary, during the times when you feel you are making the least progress, We are moving you forward. Jesus wants you to be at peace. He wants you to radiate peace. You must pray often, little dove, and We will put this peace into your heart. Your smile will reflect Us, your heavenly friends, and many will find consolation there. I am with you in a special way during this time and will watch over you closely. Speak to your other heavenly friends also, for assistance. What great graces are available to our children who are paying attention and desire to serve Us. No soul with such a desire, no matter how small and weak, will be left without complete protection. Your mother is with you and remains by your side."*

I was considering Mary's meeting of Jesus, during the Stations of the Cross, and Jesus said, *"When you look upon the face of My mother, no sacrifice is too great. Her sweetness and goodness strike deeply into your heart, and you determine that mountains may move, but you will not disappoint this good and holy woman. My chosen souls must rely on Mary, the Mother of God, to a greater degree during these times. She is making herself available in an extraordinary way right now, for the help of her little children. Be humble and ask your mother for help. She will not disappoint you. She will lead you directly to My Sacred Heart, wherein souls are confirmed in grace, as you have been confirmed in grace.* (Do write that, please.) *Fear will leave you and a firmness of intention will pervade your actions. My mother wants to lead her children and she has been given every permission from the Father in heaven."*

The Blessed Mother adds: *"My heart aches for my little ones. I see them twisting and turning in despair. How I hover near them, waiting for them to glance at me so that I may rush in to comfort and guide them. Alas, they look everywhere but to heaven. It was never this way to such a degree in the world. People are ashamed to ask God for help because they feel it is a sign* of weakness. They fear trust. They think it makes them like children. So it does. And that is what they must be to enter in the Kingdom of heaven, which is their eternal home. We must help souls to realize that it is time to come back to Jesus now. Time is short. There is no other way to say that. I want all souls to convert in the silence of their hearts and Jesus and I will lead them by the hand. No harm shall come upon them if they turn to Us in their hearts. My heart is soft and forgiving. Like any good mother, I forget the mistakes of my children almost immediately. I can help poor sinners to forgive themselves and seek the forgiveness of my Son, a forgiveness that heals and strengthens. Sinners must not be afraid. They must simply close their eyes and say, 'God, I have made mistakes. I'm sorry. I am Your child, though, and seek to be united to You.' My child, all of heaven weeps for joy when even one soul makes this act of humility and love. How We rush in to assist this soul, and protect him from the attacks of the evil one. We nurture and guide this soul until he is back walking the path to Christ with confidence. Don't be afraid, dear souls. You will find no recriminations. Only love. Be reconciled to the loving heart of my Son, who will lead you to the Father. What joy will be mine, to see you safely with Jesus."

Today at Mass, Jesus told me to come home directly, instead of doing the Stations of the Cross. He wanted me to write. I asked Him if I could do my housework first and He said, *"Yes. Complete your duties first."*

I am trying to be careful because the Blessed Mother has asked me not to be on the computer in the mornings, stating that my children need me. This morning, I came in to check my mail quickly and three times the computer would not start. It got to a certain point in the start up and froze. In frustration I rebooted and tried again, and again. Only then did it strike me that The Blessed Mother was making a point.

This morning after Communion Jesus said, *"You must try to obey immediately and completely. Your mother wishes to guide you and form you. In the future, obey with purity of spirit."* Again, feeling like two inches tall, I hurriedly agreed and tossed up an apology.

Jesus: *"Begin with My Passion. If souls would immerse themselves in My Passion, once a day, they would begin to develop a greater love for Me. Love is sacrifice. The present world sees sacrifice as something negative. This causes divorce, because the moment someone is asked to make sacrifices for another, they become outraged and feel they are being treated unjustly. This is not the case. Sacrifice brings its own rewards and forms the character of a person into holiness. Even in the case of parental sacrifice, people object. As such, many children are left abandoned and neglected. This grieves Me. This angers My Father. Children are a gift, indeed, the greatest gift, and the world wishes to throw them away. We must remind humanity that life comes from God and God decides when the earthly sojourn will end. In the case of suicide, often the person is being led by darkness. My mercy is complete. Console others with the reality of the endless depth of God's mercy. Never fear for a soul who has died. Pray for them and do not forget them. But you must tell souls that they should never fear for the salvation of loved ones. Their prayers alone at times are sufficient for the heart of their loved one to turn to Me with remorse. My heart melts instantaneously and I take them to My breast, never to be parted. Reflect with happiness on the mercy of your Jesus and the compassion of your heavenly comrades. Remember that your brothers and sisters in heaven walked your paths of conversion. There is nothing new in this world in that respect. The only new occurrence is the level of darkness, which I seek to dispel now. Be at peace and let your heart be filled with My light. There are those who wish to help you in your mission, My little one. You know who they are because they are coming to you in various ways. Use them. You sense I am smiling. It makes me happy to see My children working together and loving each other. My blessing is upon you."*

Help me never to be afraid, Lord, but to always be cautious.

This day is beginning with sickness and pain, but a light spirit. How joyful is the service of our God. Truly, His yoke is easy and His burden is light in that the closer you get, the greater your desire to serve. Indeed, the lightness of spirit is present in our Lord's service and prayer restores the buoyancy of the soul so that one proceeds joyfully. I am not cut out for martyrdom. I don't mind complaining when necessary. But Jesus makes you smile. So it would be fakery to have a sad face because you are sick. Such courage is required to begin a day at times, when you feel sick. But when you have practiced depending on Jesus, you get better at it. You then have the courage to begin difficult days or tasks because your experience assures you that Jesus will be not only walking with you, but sharing and sometimes completely shouldering the weight of your cross. Every morning you must wake and think, God has work for me. There is something terribly important I must do today for Him. I have been placed here particularly for this day and these tasks. This morning, feeling cheerfully ill, I said, "Lord, I might not get much accomplished today."

He replied: *"Slow down. Work steadily. Yesterday you accomplished a great deal, but today you will accomplish much more important work. Sometimes your tasks have to do more with loving. You could remain in bed all day but have loved much and achieved greater things than on a day when you ran from one task to another with a rapidly beating heart. My creatures were meant to move steadily. The world seems to be demanding that you move quickly. Refuse this gambit by the evil one. If you are forced to move frantically through your days, that is a sign that I want your life to change. This is important dear souls. Be advised. I want your life to move more slowly. I want you to be recollected with Me through your day. Every day, always. 'This is not possible, Jesus,' you protest. But dear child, all things are possible with Me. Slow down. You cannot love if you are running. Too many of My children are running through their lives and no longer see their loved ones, even while they are in their presence. Be with the people who are in your presence. Listen to them. Just listening to a person creates calmness. The decision to listen forces you to stop talking. Your mind might continue to race for a few moments but ask Me to steady you and I will do that. I will stop the frantic chasing of your thoughts so that you can leave your little pile of problems with Me, where they belong, and love someone whom I have chosen to walk through life with you, if only briefly. I want My love to fill this world. I want to begin a worldwide endeavor which begins with each of you. Love each person with whom I place you today. The smaller, more powerless, and more damaged they are, the more I want them to see Christ shining out at them from YOUR eyes. Only in this way will I be put back in My rightful place. Be warned. The evil one, looking at you from the eyes of some of your brothers and sisters, will identify Me within you. You will be the object of derision at times. How those opportunities delighted My saints. Practice that attitude and these same opportunities will delight you also. This is My promise to you, dearest ones. Walk with Me, live with Me, and you will no longer feel any stings this world attempts to inflict upon you. They will bounce from you like so many pointless arrows. Are you listening, My children? I want this from you. Do not disappoint Me and all joy will be yours. Your Jesus loves you and speaks directly to your hearts at this time. Listen for Me. I am there, with you."*

Our Mother adds: **"See the beauty of my Son's plan? Do you not feel it in your hearts, little children? There is no room for sadness and despair when you walk toward heaven, only happiness and hope, regardless of your earthly concerns. We are in every cross you carry. Jesus' plan is perfect and allows for every eventuality. You may question Him at times, my small ones, but never doubt Him. You will know no disappointment if you follow Us. Jesus is concerned about the fastness of today's world. It provides distraction and causes the spirit to move constantly, never pausing and recollecting itself. This is why so many of our children struggle with anxiety. Remember that anxiety never comes from God and is a sure sign that something is amiss in the way you are living. We seek to change this now. You chosen ones are the beginning of Our movement of silence, peace, and love. What you feel in your heart right now is my gift to you. Be joyful, my little ones. Your mother is with you and loves you immeasurably."**

Thoughts
on Spirituality

–5–

Tuesday June 24, 2003
Jesus

I want My chosen souls to reflect on the value of obedience. Only through obedience can I bring about the movement toward perfection within you. Your current world scoffs at obedience. Even children do not obey their parents and are not punished for their transgressions. I want My souls to be obedient and they will see their faith bloom like a flower. Truly, I will reward them in an unparalleled manner during these times.

I want to point out that souls, while being disobedient in matters of faith, are obedient to the impulses and cravings of their bodies. Your bodies are making slaves of you, dear chosen souls. It must not continue. You must bring your bodies under submission so that your soul will be freed to contemplate matters of faith. Do you want to be with Me? I am here for you. But you must clear the path for Me. You must listen for Me. To do that, dear chosen souls, you must free yourselves from these attachments that hold you under submission. I am with you, and will fight these battles for you, if only you will let Me. This is what it means to be My follower. You need worry over nothing. I will fight your battles for you and bring others to heaven through you. I can place the most beautiful, heavenly thoughts in your souls if only you will let Me. How I stand by, little soul, ready to bring you closer. Say yes to Me and we will begin our journey in earnest.

Tuesday June 24, 2003
Blessed Mother

Jesus is waiting for you, my little one. I will help you, and show you the way. Pray more, even when you do not feel like praying. Pray always, even if it is just a simple sentence, a simple thought. We are slaves to your prayers, my dear little struggling souls. We hear a plea from you and We hasten to provide every assistance. Look closely for the answers to your prayers and you will find them. Never be fooled into thinking your prayers fall on deaf ears. We work quietly and sometimes Our time is not like earthly time. But we hear your pleas and share in your concerns. Be certain that We have the answers. They are here for you and We will not leave you without guidance. Spend little time discussing problems with others. Often it is best if you listen to others. When you have a problem, come to me, your heavenly mother, and I will listen to you and help you find the best solution. You are not alone, my little ones. We long to help you and listen carefully to your petitions. The nicest prayers are the prayers of humble acceptance. You are right when you think that sometimes God must make decisions for your well being and those things we cannot change. Acceptance moves you closer to God in a swift and beautiful manner. Strive for that always, but do not be afraid to ask for anything you want or need. Above all, We will give you peace in this journey. Our heavenly companionship provides you with a quiet certainty that you walk in the light and toward the light. Do you feel it, my little one? Truly, I am with you today, asking for your obedience to my Son. You will not be disappointed, little soul of my heart.

Wednesday June 25, 2003

I was checking something with Jesus and by way of explanation I said, "Jesus, I'm just making sure. It would be a bad thing to think you were hearing the voice of God and be wrong." He replied, *"That would be a bad thing but it's not happening to you, so write."* This makes me laugh.

Jesus

I want to eradicate fear in My children. Fear chokes off holy instincts because My children do not want to be known as too holy. The worldly standard holds many hostage. I can completely erase your fear if you begin to trust Me in small things. Make many decisions during the day that you will not fear and offer those decisions to Me in the spirit of abandonment. You will see a change. Little by little you will develop a habit of trusting Me in all things. You will then be free to cast your mind into your day like one of My original disciples. Do not become disheartened by these spiritual tasks, My children. Holiness is a process, and, as with most things, I could exert My divinity and make you saints, but what merit would you gain from that? Better that My little ones make small acts of love so that I can see your wills turning toward Me. I will then move you swiftly to heights you have only imagined. Trust Me. You will not be disappointed. My children hoping to become saints, and that must be all of you, should read Scripture. Do not become discouraged with your weaknesses. You will see in Scripture that My chosen twelve had many great struggles before the Spirit came upon them in a spectacular way. It will be the same for you. You need only worry that you consistently turn your will to Me. I need many of you now, to turn to Me with abandonment. Will you say "yes" to your Jesus? Look upon My figure on the cross and remember that Jesus said "yes" for you. You are cherished, dear ones. Do not be afraid. Only trust Me.

Wednesday June 25, 2003
Blessed Mother

Like any habit, little children, trust will come easily after only a short time of practicing. I will help you. Take my hand and let me lead you. I do not want worldly fear to keep my children from reaching their rightful places in heaven. The world makes you think you have much to lose by holiness. You must scoff at this notion, children, because you have much to gain. It is the world that forces you to sacrifice much. Nothing is gained through worldliness except heartache, loneliness, and coldness toward each other. So many suffer today because the hearts of those close to them are cold. You are placed with your family members to love them and help them in their journey to Christ. Do not turn your back on those you are destined to love. If you turn to Jesus, He will place such love in your heart that it will spill over onto all you meet. There will never be a shortage of love in you and loving will become a joy, not a burden or chore. As you hear my words, child, do you not feel love in your heart? That is only the smallest example of what Jesus and I will do for you if you continue to walk Our way. Truly, the world will change through your love. Be at peace. You are loved and protected. Your mother will help you, my little children, and we will practice trusting Jesus.

Thursday June 26, 2003
Jesus

Often My words fall on deaf ears. Truly there are those who see but do not see, who hear but do not hear. These brothers and sisters will have to answer for their disregard of My graces. My words bounce off them like so many stones. You, My children, have been given the grace to hear with both your ears and your hearts. Therefore you must heed My words. My Spirit will come upon you and you will know what I want from you. Please, hear the voice of your God in your heart and respond to Me with determination. My yoke is easy and My burden is light. My true followers know joy and peace and it is reflected in their eyes. Look to one another for support during this time. These holy friendships are My gift to you, dear children, to help you walk My path during a time when there are few on that course. Listen to My words and let Me begin to use you to further My plan. My plan is one of love and salvation for your dark world. The next generation will know Me in a different way. You will be grateful to Me for this opportunity to serve.

Thursday June 26, 2003
Blessed Mother

You are responding to my Son. How happy you make your mother. Together we shall walk this path of conversion, in silence and love. See how your hearts have changed already, my children? How great is our God, that He spends such time leading His children back to Him. He is patient and good and you must also be patient and good. Look up to heaven with gratitude and joy today because your God has chosen you to implement His heavenly plan. The angels and saints stand ready to assist you in your needs. You must never be afraid, little ones. We will never leave you.

Friday June 27, 2003
Jesus

Paul of Tarsus suffered for Me. He, being a chief persecutor, lost his vision in one instant. In another instant, I returned it to him. You must not worry about your health. I can bestow good health upon you if I wish you to have it. There are times when it is more important for the coming of My Kingdom that you suffer. When the Spirit rested upon Paul, he was willing to suffer for Me and to do anything necessary to convert souls. You must work for this same feeling. My little chosen souls of this day have a hard time with both suffering and patience. Remember, My time is perfect. If We were to change over and do things according to your desires, it would not be My plan but yours. Remember how your life felt without Me, little soul, and renew your pledge to serve Me, not yourself. My time is perfect. All will occur as it should but I need souls to convert and be faithful now. The graces available to you are unlimited but that is because of the times. And the times demand full conversion and obedience. When I tell you to trust Me, I need you to at least try. We will help you along with trust as it is difficult when it is not a habit. But you must try. All day today, My little frightened child, you must tell Me you trust Me. And by the end of this day, I will place trust within you.

Friday June 27, 2003
Blessed Mother

We are making great strides with your souls, little ones. Even the smallest effort on your part is being rewarded greatly. It is important that you let go of many worldly concerns now and concern yourself with following God's will in your life. There will always be something to distract you from prayer. To follow those distractions away from prayer is like leaving the path. If you know your destination, truly, children, you must stay on the road that leads you there. The road may seem rocky and difficult at first but that is no reason to change your destination. It is the road you must travel to come to me, my little ones. I am here. Do not be afraid. I will lead you to Jesus and you will be happy and filled with gratitude for the way Jesus is calling you. Your difficulties will seem as nothing to you then. Persevere with trust. It will come to you. Again I tell you that you must practice. Do not expect great holiness without effort but your smallest efforts are being rewarded now. Look at the many, many souls who are following the world's ways and will be lost if God's chosen children do not respond. Let your hearts melt at the thought of this, my little ones and help your mother to bring them all back safely to Jesus. It is this that we work for and this that we desire. Be at peace because your mother loves you and will always protect you.

Saturday June 28, 2003
Jesus

Again you feel the weight of My cross. You must not think that because you know weariness or discouragement, that you do not serve Me well. Indeed, it is often at these times that I count you as the elect. Be like Peter, who, when asked if he was going to leave Me, replied, "Lord, You are the one true God. Where would we go?" Since your search is over and you have found the one true God, be at peace. God will not let you go. You will persevere. But you must continue to work on trusting Me, your Jesus. The times you feel discouraged and unable to serve, are the times you are depending on yourself. Dearest little children, we speak to you with such love and hope. Consider prayer like eating and drinking. How careful you are to feed your body and care for its whims. You rest often, so as not to feel physical weariness. My chosen souls must pay at least this much attention to their souls and often more. I want you to serve Me in a great way. That means you must be very small and quiet so your Jesus can speak to you and guide you. I will care for your temporal needs if you turn them over to Me. Your world must be changed and My children must work with Me for this to happen. Often, looking on your world through My eyes, you feel sickened. That is why I am intervening, children. You must trust your Jesus. Read the Gospels. You will find only love and understanding from Me. I do not come as a judge, but a merciful friend, who sees your pain and is going to give you relief. Be a servant of Me, your God, and not the world. Particularly now, during these times, you must turn your eyes to heavenly goals. Look around the world now with the eyes of a chosen soul and you will see Me working. Have faith and surround yourself with heavenly people and conversations. Speak with joy of your faith and peace. When you feel the weight of the cross, smile, because it is then that you are most united with Me.

Saturday June 28, 2003
Blessed Mother

I am with you, dear child. I see your suffering and Mother will see that you have everything you need to cope. Pray and I will intercede for you in every way necessary so that you can continue to serve your family properly. Jesus loves you so. He is so grateful that you have accepted your sufferings so bravely. You must not be sad because you need help. Dear little child of my heart, this is how we bring you to nothing so that Jesus can fill you even more. We do not judge you when you falter, but rush in to assist you. When you think of the saints suffering, know that they often faltered. This is why they were humble. If they suffered heroically from the beginning, with no effort or practice, it would not have been difficult, hence it would not have been a great cross. Do you understand? Becoming a saint is not about the finished product, little one, but about the process of becoming. It is in the process of becoming that the world is burned from you and heaven takes over. You are involved in a process and We are helping. The more you pray, the more We will be able to move you forward. Little one, be assured that the only way to your destination is the rocky road. But soon you will fly over the stones, not feeling the work. It is only briefly that you struggle so badly. And always remember that these difficult times pass and you then have an easy time. My heart aches so tenderly with love for you. I am holding you closely and your bitter tears are my personal business. I am counting them, my dear little child, and will see that they bring you great glory later. Be brave and go about your day with a joyful smile, because you have been chosen to serve Jesus in a beautiful way.

Thoughts
on Spirituality

–6–

Monday June 30 2003
Jesus

I want My children to have spiritual discipline. This means you practice your faith regardless of how you feel. There is far too much time spent on feelings today. Duty is more important. My children of the world think that their duties should be suspended if their feelings change. This is not the case, My children. On the contrary, you must complete your duties despite feelings of fatigue, boredom, and restlessness. The enemy uses these feelings to persuade people that they should not serve their loved ones. The world encourages this and does not hold people responsible when they shirk their duties or become lax or lazy. Indeed, even in work, My children complain and think they should be given liberty. They begrudge doing their duty in every area of their lives. Only in their personal entertainment do they stop complaining, and that is being taken to excess. Children, this is not the way I intended for you to live. Your duty is holy and in it you will find your path to holiness. When you are unsure about what I want you to do at a given moment, look for your duty. Does it lie with your children, your job, your family, your home, your work? Everyone has a duty and in it you will find the path to your salvation. I want you to have discipline now. Decide, through prayer and conversation with Me, what spiritual practices you need to adopt. Then you must be disciplined about these practices. Only on rare occasions should you lift your obligation to complete them. Please don't think I do not understand the pressures in your life. I am attempting, though, to realign your priorities and place them into an order that is more consistent with your decision to serve Me. You must listen to Me, and together, We will accomplish this task. You will proceed more peacefully and purposefully afterwards. I am with you and will help you to obtain this spiritual discipline, which will speed you in your conversion.

Monday June 30 2003
Blessed Mother

My children must understand that very quickly your duty becomes joyful. You have witnessed this, my little one, with your duties as a mother and wife. When you are serving Jesus in your day, the smallest, humblest task becomes an opportunity for love and the saving of souls. It does not matter what you are called upon to do. It does not matter one small bit. In this way a street sweeper is as exalted as a captain of industry. And to Us, your heavenly friends, the street sweeper might have a better opportunity to achieve great holiness. Please do not wish for worldly acclaim right now. Yes, you should be good at your job, do your best, and be joyful about the gifts God has given you. But I want your purpose to be serving God and helping your brothers and sisters. It is through this course that you will become saints, my little ones, and that is what We want for you. You see that Jesus is concerned about His children doing their duty. Pay close attention now to your duties, both in the world, and in the spiritual sense. Pray, pray, and pray, children, because through prayer, you will see God's path open up to you in a beautiful fashion. Do not begrudge Jesus your humble little tasks throughout the day. Offer them to Him with joy and a light, giving heart. He will reward you more than you can imagine and your spiritual life will take over, guiding your thoughts and actions in a remarkable way. This is where We are going with your conversion, dear ones. You will see how easy and joyful is your service to God when you proceed this way. Your mother is with you and is helping you in everything. Be at peace.

Tuesday July 1, 2003
Jesus

My smallest children do not know Me. In times past, much emphasis was placed on the religious formation of the young. In this way, all grew to adulthood with clearly formed ideas about who I was and why it was best to serve Me. They were also warned about the dangers of drifting away from Me and turning to the world for pleasure and gratification. Children are defenseless now. They do not have the knowledge necessary to protect themselves from the call of the world and the call to sin. They are tossed about by those who would like to see their souls lost. Because of this spiritual ignorance and lack of preparation, My children wander aimlessly. They are without a compass, so to speak, and feel an emptiness that they cannot fill. The effort to fill this emptiness often leads them to trouble and danger. Parents must do better. I realize that many of these parents themselves have not had the proper formation and I will take that into account when they are judged. That is why it is necessary for My chosen ones to evangelize. The Good News must be shared with all souls. What is the message, My children? I want you to tell souls everywhere that Jesus loves them. It is very simple. I love them. I want them to be with Me. I want to protect them and insulate them from the dangers of this current world. Man does not deserve the exorbitant mercy I am lavishing upon him. But I am all love and My heart aches with compassion for these souls who have been left for the world to rear and form. My dear chosen souls, you really do not know how filled with joy We are when We see a family providing their children with the proper formation. We give every assistance and will use these children to be spiritual leaders later. Your job is important to Us. I cannot stress that enough. Parents, you must take your duty very seriously right now as We need this. Never feel concerned. You need only live a simple life and pray. Everything else will be accomplished by Me, with the help of My mother and the angels and saints. I need you now, chosen souls. We have loved each other in the past. Do not disappoint Me.

Tuesday July 1, 2003
Blessed Mother

Little children, hear my Son. How eager He is to help you and bring you back safely to Him. Do not fear, please, if you have made mistakes. We are only concerned about today and this must be your approach also. Be sorry for your sins and walk away from them. Often, the evil one will attempt to keep you tied to past sins by reminding you of them and trying to persuade you that sinners cannot be true chosen souls. How ridiculous a notion! Look to the Bible for proof. Jesus came for sinners. Jesus will return for sinners. And my little chosen souls will prepare the way for Him. I am counting every one of you who receives this message as a chosen soul. What joy will be yours. Think about joy, dear little child. When did you last feel joy? Your mother will show you heavenly joy if you heed Our messages now. Don't be afraid, my small ones. Holiness is a process and it is mostly up to Jesus to move you through that process. In a special way, right now, you can let Jesus form you. We are going to take care of everything. You need only love Jesus and let Him direct your life. Be like a small sparrow, living only in the moment, confident that God will provide everything needed for the next day, the next season, and the next year. Your mother blesses you.

Wednesday July 2, 2003
Jesus

My children rely too often on the thoughts of others. Children, you must think for yourself. The opinions of others are often flawed and have a worldly origin. Of what use is that to you? I want you to spend your time quietly, as much as possible. Do not discuss every aspect of your life. It is not necessary and often leaves you distracted and upset. Your energy is wasted in this way and there is that much less remaining for prayer. Focus your strength and energy on serving Me in your day. Before you speak, ask yourself if what you are going to say is of value. Before you offer an opinion, be certain you have given this thought consideration. Do not lead others astray, as I am warning you not to be led astray. Silence is necessary now, as We have said. Useless conversations add to the constant din of noise that leaves the spirit no peace. You will not understand what I need from you, dear children, unless you are quiet and thoughtful. Also, this quietness encourages My Spirit to rest within you, and you will feel that presence. You will then speak with authority and correctness. And you will begin to offer opinions and counsel that have value and direction, instead of merely adding to the noise of this present world. Be at peace now, in all of your troubles. I want My children to move through their days with confidence, even if they are carrying crosses for Me. The heavier the cross, dear ones, the closer I will be. Do not fear. You will not be left in the wilderness. I call My own to Me and My own know Me.

Wednesday July 2, 2003
Blessed Mother

You see that Jesus is leaving nothing to chance. He wishes to guide His children in an unusual way during this time. All has been foreseen, dear children. I want you to say "no" to anxiety and distress. My children can rest peacefully in my arms these days, as Jesus fulfills His plan for the salvation of the world. How happy you will be to have participated. Jesus is granting you great graces, by asking for your help. I know you will not disappoint Him. All you need to do to serve Him is be at peace and listen to His voice in prayer. Be still, little ones, and know that He is God. All else, all details, will flow naturally from that one directive. Do you hear the voice of your mother, little one? I am appealing to your heart and beg you to trust me and live my words. These are serious times, but I am with you, and will quiet all of your fears. Be at peace now, and spend your time with Jesus in your heart.

Thursday July 3, 2003
Jesus

Again, today, I speak to souls. My children, you will recognize Me in your life when you begin to follow Me. Look for Me and My desires as you go through your day. View everything as an opportunity for holiness. View everything as an opportunity to be closer to Me. Do not be short tempered with your brothers and sisters in the world. They are also My children and it hurts Me when you judge them so harshly. I have given you many gifts. I will expect an accounting for them. You, My chosen children, are called to a higher level of holiness than others. You have everything you need to achieve the level I desire. This is not going to be difficult if you are heeding My words. Indeed, you will find your life will become simpler, easier, and more joyful as you begin to follow Me. Your life is not intended to be complex. God would not have created a complex world, destined to confuse His children. Your Father in heaven is not like that. Read the Bible, My children, and you will come to know your God. He is all love. He sees to everything for you. Life is intended to be simple, beautiful, and you are to be learning always. The modern world tries to persuade you to think that life is complex. Most issues are simple. For example, abortion is murder, dear ones. Do not be fooled. Children are your treasure, regardless of when your heavenly Father decides to send them. That issue is not complex and I need My children to be courageous in defending the lives of the unborn children of God. Your generation is suffering untold calamites because of this grave, grave sin. Be alert, My children, and I will instruct you in your role. But truly I say to you, all of heaven cries out against this crime. How long can your God remain silent in the face of these pleas? I am with you. I love you. I will remain with you in a special way and anything you are asked to do for Me, will be accompanied by such graces that it will be easy to accomplish. But you must remain close to Me. It is only when you drift off and close your ears to Me that your life becomes complex again. Be happy, dear ones. All of heaven stands ready to assist you.

Thursday July 3, 2003
Blessed Mother

I am one of the voices pleading with God to intervene for the protection of my unborn children. I cannot describe the grief this situation has caused me. Be strong, little children. You must represent Jesus in your world. This sin has occurred because there are so few representing my Son. We told you that people must see Jesus looking out at them from your eyes. This is true. If there were enough people following my Son, the crime of abortion would never have happened. There are not enough representatives of Christ in the world to properly combat this outrage. But that is changing, as I have said. The world is turning to God. In pain and despair the world seeks relief. And God, in His all encompassing love and mercy, is responding. No longer will God allow His children to be victimized. Be happy, my dear ones. God is changing your world and His justice will insure that the children of light be allowed to follow their God in the world He created. Your mother is with you and protects you.

Friday July 4, 2003
Jesus

I wish to draw souls out of the world. As the world lured them away from Me, now I call them back. My Sacred Heart, which beats with love for My children, is crying out with love. Many of My children will heed the call of My heart and follow Me. They will bring souls with them. This is the beginning of My Renewal and events will follow each other. The enemy is weakening as more souls return to the light. My children initially find it difficult to leave the emptiness of the world. Emptiness becomes a habit and the materialism that people use to fill the emptiness also becomes a habit. But I offer something so sparkling, so eternal, and so pristine, that the soul longs for it. I offer goodness and happiness. I offer peace and above all I offer love. My love is real. If you want to see examples of My love, children, before you make the decision to come back to Me, look to My chosen souls. See how they love each other and sacrifice for each other. You will not find constant harsh words and recriminations between them. You will see them bearing with each other in patience and tolerance. My chosen souls are doing their duty. That is another way to recognize them. They work in the world, they care for their family members, they tell the truth, and when they make mistakes they provide recompense. Look to the lives of My chosen souls for example. They often become bored and discouraged, like My children still wandering, but they persevere and the troublesome feelings pass. Their souls are strengthened by their triumph over these temptations. My chosen souls have troubles, just like others. But watch closely how they respond to their troubles. They help each other, they appeal to Me, their God, and they accept their crosses. You will find goodness in the eyes of My chosen souls. Do you want that to be yours? Come back to Me. The world offers you nothing. The world does not love you. Indeed, you will find only rejection and hatred in the world. Come back to Me and begin to examine your inheritance, which is goodness, love and eternal security and joy.

Thursday July 4, 2003
Blessed Mother

Jesus calls out with such passion and love. Little ones, feel the love in His words. He is feeling so strongly the absence of so many souls wandering lost in the darkness of the world. I, too, ache for these souls. Be careful never to discard a soul for lost. Try, try, and try to call them back. I realize that souls in trouble can be very hurtful to my children. I do not want that and will protect you if you appeal to me. Often, you should love them and pray for them, leaving them to Jesus. Remember that with many souls, your good wishes and prayers are enough to save their souls from perdition. So do not fear. Be at peace, always, in these situations, and let your heavenly friends intervene. Your love can feel like a cross at these times, and so it is, dear children. Love can be a burden, but that creates strength in your soul. Remember always that Jesus has a plan. It is the best plan for you and your loved ones and He will deal with souls who refuse His graces and follow the paths of darkness. You need only be responsible for your own soul, and the formation of any children under your care. If your children choose darkness, pray for them, and appeal to me. I will help you with your children. That is my promise to you. As a mother, I understand a mother's great love and concern. Also, if you feel you have made mistakes with your children, appeal to me. I will intercede for you before the Heavenly Throne of our Father and provide them with mitigation for your faults. In this way, the children will not reap the whole harvest of your flaws. Do you see how We love you? Do you see how We compensate for your mistakes and flaws? We are all love, little ones. We are all acceptance of your humanity and of the difficulties you are having in this world filled with distortions. There is only one way now, and it is Our way. Come back to the Sacred Heart of my Son. You will find only love, acceptance, and joy. Your mother remains with you and is ever ready to assist you.

Saturday July 5, 2003
Jesus

I would speak to souls today about the value of obedience. My chosen ones believe they should understand everything. This is not always possible. There are times when you must obey Me without understanding why I have chosen to ask a thing of you. I realize this is difficult for you, and that is why I am asking you to practice this virtue. There will come a time when I ask you for obedience and I will need an immediate response. I cannot have My chosen ones wasting time, questioning why I am asking them to complete a task. So now We will practice obedience, dear ones. In your everyday life, I want you to always consider what it is that Jesus is asking from you. You will know, in your heart, what My desires require. Please, begin this today and practice obeying immediately, even though perhaps you do not recognize the merit of the request. How often you will say later, I see now, why My Jesus asked me to do that task. Children, in this way you will become free. Your liberty will be complete and your slavery to this world will end. I need obedient servants. Again, I tell you, study the Bible. Read the Gospels. My children in the past did not always under-

stand why they were asked to do things. Even My mother, Mary, did not always understand the value of her actions. Saint Joseph, My foster father, is a beautiful example of the reverence a soul must possess for the Divine Will in his life. Ask St. Joseph to help you with obedience and the trust necessary to obey. He will hear you. And you will progress. This is a time, now, for heeding My messages, children. I say this with all solemnity. Be advised. Your God wishes to save you through your obedience.

Saturday July 5, 2003
Blessed Mother

How well my children are listening in these days. Your mother is pleased with you, dear ones, because you are beginning to heed the words of my Son. We are helping you and stand by to help you still more. How the soul groans with these initial efforts. I know you feel the pains of growth and I know this is often difficult. Be brave, little souls. Believe Us when We say that your difficulties will be short-lived. And if you could see the banquet that awaits you, there would be no hesitation. We must ransom as many souls as possible now. Think of your sufferings as nothing. Remember, it is likely that a soul suffered for your conversion. At the very least, gaze on your crucifix and see the cost of your final redemption. Jesus counts it as nothing. Willingly He would do it again for you. He loves you, dear little ones. Jesus intends to reward you more than you can imagine for your obedience. And practicing will make it seem effortless. It becomes a habit and you give it very little thought after that. Be at peace always and show others how happy is the service to Christ.

Thoughts
on Spirituality

–7–

Monday July 7, 2003
Jesus

It is crucial that souls listen to Me. I want to lead them to the light. The enemy seeks to lead them away from the light. How I suffer because of this. Children, you must understand that you can no longer compromise with the world. Compromise is causing souls to be lost. If you, My chosen souls, respond to Me in a half-hearted, lukewarm way, We will never save the souls who are being batted about the world like so many embers from a fire. No. We must do better now. I want you to turn your eyes up to heaven and pledge your allegiance to My Father, who is all love. He will accept your pledge and consider you as soldiers of the light. Only then can we commence this Rescue Mission. Consider that there are many souls, destined to be saved by you, through your sacrifices and loyalty to Me. Child of My heart, those souls will be lost. You will grieve them and mourn your lack of faith and diligence. I do not want to frighten My children but I must convey to you the seriousness of these times. We are releasing countless graces now, to assist you in the preparation for the coming of God's Kingdom. Be counted as a follower of Christ during these times and you will live forever in the love that surrounds Me. You may say fearfully, "Lord, what can I do? I am only one person." Remember that there is no price for one soul. If one soul is worth dying for, and this is the truth, then how important is it that you respond to Me wholeheartedly so that I can save many through you? Truly, the graces at your disposal are countless. Your "yes" to Me today unleashes all manner of graces and sets into motion the saving of many souls who are being called from the darkness, now, as I am calling you. I am looking for quietness. I am looking for a calm defense of God. I am looking for consistent service and prayer. I am not calling you from the world. It is I who put you in the world, little children, and I intend to use you right where I have placed you. Move with confidence through your days and understand that it is I, your Jesus, your God, who is asking for your help. Do not turn your back on Me, dear one, for I love you and wish to save you.

Monday July 7, 2003
Blessed Mother

You can see that my Son is suffering. And I suffer with Him. We suffer because many souls are throwing away their opportunity to spend eternity in the light that is heaven. Little souls, your mother is anxious to help you now. Please respond with love and be consistent in your prayer lives. Again we must warn you that your feelings do not constitute reality. We do not rewrite all of history because you are discouraged for a day. You must accept your discouragement as part of your cross. On another day, you will feel better, and you will be so glad that you persevered and served Christ well on the day you did not feel as holy. Try to understand that We want your service every day, regardless of how you feel. On some days, of course, you will do better than others. This is to be expected and should not upset you. But mostly, We wish you to set prayer goals and keep to them. Do not think that the merit of your prayer is based on how you feel when you are praying. You may feel nothing on some days, but you must persevere and believe me when I tell you that on those days, when you feel nothing, you are saving as many souls through your smallest prayers, as on the days when all of heaven seems open to you. Smile now, and let everyone you meet see the smile of Jesus. You are a soul who is being held close to my heart. My child, my little one, how precious you are to me.

Take these words and be docile while they change your life. Your mother will see to everything for you, but you must pray.

Tuesday July 8, 2003
Jesus

Today, again, I call out to My chosen souls. Dear one, I am calling you to serve Me. Do not fear that I am calling you to complete an impossible task. Again I tell you that anything I ask of you will be made easy for you. I do not want my little souls failing to serve Me because they are afraid. Believe Me when I say that My plan is perfect and it is the best possible plan for you. All circumstances have been addressed in advance for you by My Divine Providence. Dearest child of My heart, of what can you possibly be afraid? Your Jesus will not abandon you. Your Jesus will not set you a task and leave you without the graces necessary to accomplish this task. I have seen to everything. You need only pray and obey. Do you refuse Me this? I want you to set an example to your brothers and sisters who have not yet returned to Me. They must see you and desire to emulate you in order to have what you have. You must have faith. Because it is then that I can place peace in your heart and it is peace that is so attractive to those still restlessly wandering through the darkness in the world. Be at peace now, in your decision to serve Me. All of heaven is watching and desires to see you succeed. You have an infinite amount of help. The evil one will be defeated, My child, and My chosen souls will be instrumental in this process. Do not be afraid that My service will cost you more than you have to give. Your Jesus calls you from the world now to take direction. You must pray and I will fill the longing in your heart.

Tuesday July 8, 2003
Blessed Mother

Dearest children, your mother wishes to assure you that all will be well. When you look toward heaven, you are not afraid. This is because you then see this world as a transient state. It is not in the world that you are destined to spend eternity, but in heaven. Therefore, my dear children, you must concern yourselves with heavenly causes and heavenly things. Dear ones, note how refreshed you feel after a conversation with a like-minded soul. Heaven is filled with souls such as these, who have fought the good fight. They are alert to the struggles on earth and the struggles you personally are having. There is great love and support for you. How anxious I am for you to serve my Son so that you will enjoy heaven. Little souls, your best imaginative dream of heaven falls far short of the reality. Such happiness will be yours. And Jesus asks only that you say "yes" to Him and be willing to serve. Your mother blesses you.

Wednesday July 9, 2003
Jesus

Today I speak to My chosen souls. Heaven awaits you, dear souls. You do not have to wait until after your death. Unity with Me is heaven, so you can experience a foretaste of heaven on the earth. As I draw you deeper into My heart, you will begin to understand why My saints lost all interest in the world, except the saving of souls. They concerned themselves with My desires only, which always placed their duty in life first. Today, My children concern themselves with all manner of nonsense. Children, you must see these things for what they are. They are a distraction from Me. The evil one wants to draw you away from prayer, from reflection, indeed, even from heaven. I am drawing you back to the light. Feel the pull of heaven as We cry out to you in warning. Your sins count as nothing to Me, dear souls, but you must repent. I am all mercy, and want only to bring you home safely. Humble yourself before Me, so that I may fill you with My graces. Be assured that I have work for you. Every soul is important and has a role to play in the coming of My Kingdom. Will you leave your work to others, dear souls? That is not what I have willed. I have placed you here, in this time, to serve

Me in a particular way. Say "yes" to Me, dear soul, and together, We will begin.

Wednesday July 9, 2003
Blessed Mother

Remember to pray, children. In this way, every action throughout your day can be sanctified. Think of all the small tasks you complete, barely giving any thought to them. If you offer them to Us with love, We can use even the smallest action for the salvation of sinners. It is time now to pay attention. Do not put Our words down and forget them. I want you to act in obedience to Our words and let them change your life. It will feel like the most natural thing in the world, this transition to holiness. Once you make the decision, begin to pray. Once you begin to pray, obedience will come naturally. After obedience, We can move you swiftly to great levels of holiness. My dear one, you will then see the coming of God's Kingdom. The more you obey, the more We can reveal to you. There are many souls who allow their lives to be led by the enemy. They are leading others after them. This must cease. Answer "yes" to your mother and feel the closeness of Jesus, my Son. He will change you and introduce great beauty to your life. Be at peace as you follow the path to holiness. We are with you, and ask only that you do your best.

Thursday July 10, 2003
Jesus

Today I plead with My children to heed My words. There are many souls in the world who only need to be invited to My table. They are softhearted souls, seeking guidance and direction. You, My chosen souls, must provide that guidance and direction. That is why you will be placed in contact with many souls. Speak My name freely and lovingly. Speak My name naturally in your conversation. Speak My name often, and do not use it to curse others. If these souls, who are directionless because of the failure of many of My children to provide that direction, hear My name spoken lovingly and respectfully, their hearts will jump up, like John the Baptist's heart jumped in his mother's womb. They will know that it is their Savior who is being spoken of so lovingly. And they will be watching you, dear soul, to see what you do, how you act, speak, and treat others. These souls, given a small bit of direction, will follow you. They will not need years of calling, as I have called to many of you for years. They seek only the correct direction and they will walk toward Me without falter. Can you imagine, My dear ones, how I grieve that so many of them are not living the life of the Christian? And can you imagine how many souls, destined to be called then by them, have been left in the world? Do you see, little ones, how every soul is so critical to My Kingdom? We do not want Our brothers and sisters abandoned, for the want of your duty being fulfilled. How blessed are you that you have been called, indeed, and given these messages. Little child, you are a Christian because some-one fulfilled their duty. Now you must ful-fill your duty and call out to others in love and solicitude. Leave nothing undone that could bring a soul to Me. Let those of the world scoff at you, if they dare. The inhabitants of heaven commend you. If you hear My name, spoken in ridicule or anger, turn away, praying to Me for the forgiveness of that person. Then, instead of your God being unwelcome and ridiculed in that situation, He will be honored. That, My child, is, in summary, what I am calling you to do. Be joyful. Be glad. You are My chosen one and My favor and Spirit rests upon you.

Thursday July 10, 2003
Blessed Mother

I am very distressed at the way my Son's name is being spoken today. Children, Jesus is your God. There is no other. The seriousness of the misuse of His name should make you quake in fear. There will be a reckoning for these grave sins, committed so flippantly in today's world. And I must tell you that a large part of the problem with this kind of talk is the damage it does with regard to the conversion of others. You do not see this but to have the name of Jesus tossed around like the most common of curse words, brings down all manner of darkness to your world. You must delight the angels of heaven, children, not the angels of darkness. Be one who will not tolerate it. I know that it offends you, as it offends me. Pray often that this will cease, children. We cannot have this anymore. Remember that all foul language is wasted language. It does nothing to further our work and often works against our work. You would not readily or willingly pull against the coming of the Kingdom of your God, dear child. So do not use foul language, because, however inadvertently, that is what you are doing. Use everything to give glory to my Son, including your beautiful language. Mother wants you to know that even these little things are very important to Us and very important to your soul and the movement of your soul to heaven. Remember that we are bringing others to heaven with us during this time. That is our goal, little souls, so let us leave no stone unturned. We will help you and if you have questions, you may ask Us. We want to guide you in this way and We will place the answer in front of you or within you. Let Us help you. Your mother wishes you only peace and blessing.

Thoughts
on Spirituality

–8–

Sunday July 13, 2003
Blessed Mother

Dear children, it is I, your mother, who speaks to you in warning. The enemy seeks to prevent this work and destroy the graces my Son is building in this soul. You must pray now, more than ever before that the will of my Son be completed. Little ones, your mother worries over your salvation. You do not realize the danger that surrounds you and presses against you. It is through Our intercession and protection that you are being insulated so that this work may continue. Be vigilant and persevere. Do not think of yourselves and your worldly desires. We must work for heaven now. I want this little cohort to set the example and to be the example. That is all for now. Your mother blesses you and remains with you but a good mother makes haste to warn her children of an unseen danger. That is what I am doing. Pray for the Coming of God's Kingdom and the success of this work. Pray the Rosary, my dear children, every day, for my intentions, which always reflect the will of my Son.

Monday July 14, 2003
Jesus

My dear children, remember that your feelings do not constitute your actions, any more than your body guides your soul. The soul must have dominion over its body or great difficulty will ensue. In the same way, My chosen souls have decided on a course of action. You have decided to serve Me, little ones. Now you must serve Me and let your feelings go where they may. What care you whether you feel up or down, high or low, as long as you stay the course and continue to follow My will in your life? You will see, upon inspection, that holy souls rose every morning and followed the course marked out by their decision to follow Me, their God. They were not changeable, like the things of this world. Children, stay the course now. Neither look to the right, nor the left. Keep My words in your heart and I will steady you. You will know My chosen ones by their consistent pattern of behavior. I do not want you coming back and forth, and to and fro anymore, like you may have in the past. We are a team now and I want to know that I can depend on you, as you can always depend on Me. When you awaken and feel badly, or awaken and feel unholy, yearning for worldly things, move with calm and determination into the day, and the feelings will change. This world is in great trouble and it is partially because mankind is ruled by his feelings from one day to the next. No longer. We have embarked on a course. Let Us move forward with constancy and determination, regardless of how We feel on a given day. Do you understand, My chosen one? You must pay no attention to your changeable feelings. Only pay attention to Me and My will for you. I bless you now and together We commence.

Monday July 14, 2003
Blessed Mother

Dear little souls, how difficult it can be for you to be in the world but not of the world. Do not think We are unsympathetic to your difficulties. Indeed, it is for this reason we encourage you to pray so steadily. Prayer must be your lifeblood. We can provide you with a steady stream of grace and goodness, of confidence and courage, if you pray often. Did you set your prayer goals? Double them. What is it I am asking of you? I am asking you children, to make prayer the constant in your life. I desire that you be in prayer always, regardless of what you are doing. If you are driving, offer it to Jesus. If you are working, offer it to Jesus. If you are performing a menial task, I can make it a heavenly accomplishment. Imagine dear child, that you can unite every task to my Son for the Coming of His Kingdom. His Kingdom is coming, little soul. And I need your help. There are stubborn souls who will stop at nothing to resist God's will and destroy His plan. We cannot have that. We must push back hard now with goodness and love. In this way, mother can reach into the world and take many children out of harm's way. My dear precious little child, someone sacrificed for you and your mother was able to protect you. Do the same. Talk to me throughout your day. That is prayer. Close your eyes and think of Jesus on the cross. Now think of Him on the cross, awake, suffering for hours.

Is it really asking so much that you remain with Him through your day, as He fills you with joy and divine consolations? Your heavenly friends are with me, urging you to be soldiers of the light, soldiers of the greatest obedience. One little step at a time, let us proceed. Do not think there has been a mistake and We are calling the wrong person. It is you We are calling. We cry out to you in love and warning and urge you now to answer this call to arms, with prayer being your weapon.

Tuesday, July 15, 2003 2:30 am
Jesus

I would speak to My children about faith on this day, as I seek to pull them closer. Dear children, let your faith rule your hearts. Again I explain to you that faith, while a gift, is also a practice, or way of life. You make a decision, saying to yourself, "I must live my life based on my faith, and because of my faith." All decisions and actions then must stem from your faith and be an offshoot of this faith. When you walk into a church on a weekday morning, that is a decision based on your faith. "I believe in God, I believe Jesus is calling me, I believe my Blessed Mother has requested my help, therefore I am going to pray on this day and every day." I am assuming this is consistent with your God-given duties. If I am not calling you to attend daily Mass or Adoration, I will tell you when I want you to pray. I refer to prayer in a church now, and structured prayer. As My mother said, you should be in a united form of prayer as often as you can throughout the day. But We are also increasing your structured prayer if it is necessary that We do so. Many of My children have stopped visiting churches. They say they can pray at home. But alas, they do not. This is yet another sign of The Great Disobedience. My children who speak this way, I am calling out to you in firmness. I did not ask you to pray at home on the Sabbath. I asked you to attend to your religious duties. When you die, and you face Me, I will ask you if you completed these duties. Woe be to those who dared to make their own rules, and superimpose those rules over the law of God. What audacity they practice. What a bad example they set for others. Again, I say, no longer. God's law will preside, children. I would have you answer immediately to Me, your God, who calls you. Look closely at your life right now. Decide prayerfully what your duty consists of in every area. Then fulfill those duties. I want no excuses. I want your duties fulfilled with enthusiasm and love. In the beginning, it is possible that this will be difficult for you. But I will be there. I do not ask you for something, little child, and then withhold the graces necessary to complete this task. It will never happen that way. You look up to heaven and say, "My God, this is too hard. I cannot do this." First, be certain that I am, in fact, asking you to do this thing. Then, sit quietly while I grant you the gift of calm, and try again. If We proceed together, My blessed little soul, you will find your task easy. This is My promise to you and if you look at My world and read My Scripture, you will find that I never broke a promise. It is something that is not even possible. I am your God. Heed My words of love and direction today.

Tuesday July 15, 2003
Blessed Mother

Little child, heed His words. He speaks with such love and wisdom. You will not find this wisdom on the earth or from an earthly source. You will not find happiness on the earth or from an earthly source. Do you want to be happy? Are you tired of being sad, discouraged, and joyless? Come back to Us now, in obedience, and We will minister to your fatigue and sadness. We will refresh you and after We have refreshed you and healed you, We will set about saving the world. You will not be alone any longer, little soul. We have complete forgiveness for you. Together we will step away, as we leave your past sins and failures behind. Take my hand, little child of my heart, and your mother will lead you to every spiritual success. Truly, you will not even believe how We intend to change your life. I want you to be a great spiritual leader. I want you to stand upright, carrying the staff of Moses, and pull my children from the smoldering spiritual ruins of this world. Do not refuse your mother's request. You will be brave and true to this calling, little child. Do not be afraid. Your strength will be given to you as a gift. So take these first trembling steps in faith and all manner of graces will flow down upon you. My motherly peace is flowing down upon you now, even as we talk together in this way. I bless you, and call you as my own.

Tuesday July 15, 2003 4pm
Blessed Mother

My dear little one, how your obedience delights me. I want to warn my children about a danger that threatens to derail their spiritual renewal. The enemy seeks to pull you off track by offering worldly delights. I want you to pray for discernment when you are faced with a fork in the road, be it in your career, your living arrangements, or your family life. I must tell you that I want to protect you and I am doing so. These attacks can be concealed under the guise of something good, but you will never be fooled if you consult Jesus and pray for discernment. Do you see, children, why your mother is beseeching you to pray in a determined fashion? If you stop and start, you give the enemy room to work and gradually you can slide further away. It is as if you are put to sleep when this happens and you become spiritually groggy. Be alert during these days of decision. Be cheerful. And above all, be vigilant with regard to the prayer goals you have set. Your mother is guiding and protecting you in an enhanced way and I send you a blessing of discernment.

Wednesday July 16, 2003 4am
Jesus

Today I want to talk about perseverance during difficult times or times of crisis. My children, it is during these times where your relationship with Me is of the greatest value. Do not forget Me when you are experiencing human exhaustion or great upheavals, including sickness. Sadly, many of even My chosen ones forget that I am with them and wish to steer them through crisis and illness. I understand. When your life changes abruptly or you feel physically unwell, it is sometimes hard to remember to practice your faith. But I tell you now that this is the time to back out of the world even more fully and let Me direct everything. If you are practicing the life of a Christ follower, this is not a long stretch for you. My graces pour down upon you during these times. You must also ask yourself always what it is that Jesus is attempting to show you through tragedy or illness. Children, I do not attempt to show you that your God is a cold and harsh Being. On the contrary, your God loves you and directs everything, often intervening to save you from the folly of your error and sin. People today, remarkably, blame God for all manner of hardship and badness. They use the fruits of sin to justify their failure to follow Me. Children, it is not I who have brought this darkness over the world. It is you, by your sin and failure to serve. There is enough food in the world. There should not be hunger. Medical care, also, can be spread around in a more effective manner. Humanitarian assistance to your poor and less advanced societies is an act of mercy and those who practice it are following My will, whether they know it or not. Truly, I want these acts of mercy from you. And I want you to stop blaming your God for your failures. Do not let others get away with this. Defend Me. And defend My priests and nuns. Vocations are down in your more advanced societies. I am sending you holy souls but you are not nurturing them. They receive no formation or direction and their gifts are not developed. Children, dear children, I need leaders now. I need every single one of you to turn your faces to heaven and agree to serve Me with your whole lives. The plan I have for you will amaze you. Be docile and let Jesus direct. Through this will come happiness and relief to so many. This will happen, My children. The darkness has lost its time now and I will have the world My way. You must see that this happens in your corner. Are you ready to walk with Me? I call you, My child. Waste no more time. Respond to Me now.

Wednesday July 16, 2003
Blessed Mother

Children, Jesus is trying to tell you gently that you must join Him now. Not later, but now. The time of darkness is mercifully near its end and Jesus is going to intervene in the world in an extraordinary fashion. You must be prepared and that is why We are sending you these messages. Do not ignore the prophets we send as an act of extended mercy. Can you imagine how you will feel if you have been warned but failed to respond? Can you ignore Jesus after He has shown you so much love? Can you continue, possibly, to turn your back on Him? Of course not. Because in your heart you know that Jesus is the Way, and you know that He calls you for the last time in this world. My children must obey their God and hasten to assist Him. Be on Our side, dear child. Our side is the side of love. Our side is the side of obedience. Our side is the side of light, happiness, and service to others. There is no real choice for you. Your God cries out to you sharply and you must answer Him. I, your heavenly mother, will help you. We are doing everything. We need only your "yes" to unleash all manner of graces upon you. Your mother blesses you and helps you in every decision, including the decision to serve. Be at peace with your service to Christ, little one, as it is the only correct decision.

Wednesday July 16, 2003 3pm
Blessed Mother

Dear little children, the world seeks to destroy your peace. You must hold on tightly to your heavenly peace. When events disturb you, no matter how trying, bring the situation to Us. There is a correct way to respond, a correct way to handle difficulties, and We will see that you have the guidance you need. This enables you to walk away from situations or people who disturb you with the knowledge that you acted in a manner consistent with your commitment to Christ. Do not think that there is any situation on this earth with which We are unfamiliar, or for which we lack the answers. This is simply not possible. This relationship we are developing with you has untold benefits and merits. One of the benefits is that We will handle your difficult moments and people. You are not alone anymore. You do not need to seek further for the answers. In all kindness, gentleness, and love, we will direct you to the holy response to all of life's dilemmas. Be at peace now, knowing that your service to the Lord entitles you to every grace and blessing. Use these graces and blessings to restore and protect your peace. Truly, I am with you, in your fatigue and struggle. Move slowly and you will not misstep.

Thursday July 17, 2003
Jesus

My, child, I speak today to all souls who have fallen away. It is time to come back to Me now. I call you. You hear My voice and you know it is I, your Jesus Christ, who calls out to you. The fact that you know My voice, tells you that you belong to Me. Because you belong to Me, little soul, you must return to Me now. I want you to repent of your sins. Call out to Me and I will hear you. I will give you exact direction on how you are to return to the fold. Dear lost one, I have heard the groaning of your soul and I am responding to your pain. The evil one makes war on the souls of My children and attempts to take them away. But the enemy offers you nothing. Only emptiness. You see that now, little soul, so return to Me. I offer you all that is beautiful, noble, and eternal. You will NEVER regret that you came back to Me. Are you listening? Are you allowing your poor troubled heart to answer Me? I am healing you. I wish to heal you even further, until your soul is as pure as necessary to enter into My Kingdom. Dear child, do you want to spend eternity with happiness, with joy in the goodness of others? I do not refer to the hypocritical goodness of some of your earthly companions. That false goodness has disappointed you in the past and is the source of some of your bitterness. Fear not. The light will shine upon that goodness and expose it for evil. I refer to real goodness that encompasses all virtue. I speak now of the virtue of courage, courage in the face of a world that despises God and all that is good. My children have been seduced by the worthless baubles of materialism, with which they adorn themselves, in an effort to feel valued. Children, it is My value you must aspire to and the world does not offer it. This value comes only from one source. Me. Jesus Christ. I am the one who died for you and I intend to save you again. I call you from the world this day and claim you for My own. I will protect you from here on, dear little prodigal soul, and your sins will be wiped away into nothingness. This is My promise to you. I will forget your sins. Come back to Me. You will never regret that you did this.

Thursday July 17, 2003
Blessed Mother

Do you hear My Son's voice? He is calling His children with authority. Dear little ones, He does this in an effort to save them. The Voice of my Son bears authority and that is why He says His children will know that it is He, their God, who calls out to them. My little ones must make a choice now. And they must choose God and all that is good. Chosen ones, it is time to pray, and you have been called upon to pray. Join your mother in this mission of mercy to your fallen brothers and sisters. Together we minister to their souls, preparing their souls to melt with love for the Divine Rescuer, who seeks them out at this time. Truly, we call you with an unparalleled urgency. You feel this in your hearts and this is an accurate, divinely placed, knowledge. Little ones, be joyful. God has chosen you to help Him and that is wonderful for you and for every soul that you reach. Through you, I will reach out to many. I am helping Jesus, with every grace available to me at this time. Much of this grace comes from your prayers and sacrifices and little offerings. So do not begrudge me these gifts. Children, I am also using, in a special way, the lives of my holy ones who are consecrated to me. Priests and religious, holy men and women, console my heart in an extraordinary fashion right now and I am maximizing the tremendous graces I receive from these righteous souls. Religious in the world are under attack. Be brave, religious souls. Your mother defends you as her own and you will be raised up to your rightful place soon. Instead of being honored by the world, you are reviled and slandered. This will not endure. I want to say that there are those religious who have disappointed my Son and turned to the evil one. Do not think, oh souls of satan, that you will escape divine justice. And for you who have damaged innocent souls? All of heaven quakes with the retribution that will be yours. I say this to you with a special gravity. Repent. Admit your sins and become cleansed. Only in this way will you enter into the Kingdom of God. Children, be reflective during these times. We are with you, and preparing the world for a marked change. I bless all of you and seek to lead you to my Son.

Thursday July 17, 2003
Blessed Mother

I want my children to begin detaching from the world. To do this, children, you must begin limiting the amount of time you spend watching television. There is no question that television has lured souls into a false world that distorts their view of reality. Very few programs depict characters who are appropriate role models for children of the light. Guidance will not be found on television and in many instances children are misled and damaged from exposure. My children, also limit your time shopping. Buy necessities and keep your focus to family and duty. Live a healthy life, limiting entertainment. Opt for prayer and reflection. Soon you will not miss these things and you will correctly count them as so many nothings. Spend time with your family, walking, talking, and enjoying those things created by God. Set an example of quietness. Study the saints and the lives of holy souls. You have a great many spiritual comrades and your number increases by the hour. Truly, you will begin to see this, and it will strengthen you. Bloom where you are planted, little soul, unless Jesus directs otherwise. I am with you, and alertly watch for a sign that you need me. Truly, your mother is close to you.

Friday July 18, 2003
Jesus

Today I speak to souls about love. Love is important. Indeed, it is the most important thing of all things. That is the reason it has become so distorted in your modern world. The side of darkness would like to see love destroyed. The modern world would put this distorted version in its place so that no one would be able to find love and their hearts would then become like ice. Many of My children are ignorant of true, genuine love. It is for this reason that children are unwelcome unless they fill a need for their parents. My dear ones, if you follow Me, you will learn about genuine love, which offers untold fruits and opportunities for growth. Marriage, for example, and I speak of a sacramental union, sanctioned and maintained by Me, provides great opportunity to learn about love, because it is a constant merging of one will to another. This demands sacrifice and compromise. You must give, give, and give to experience the Sacrament of Marriage. Your world, which has distorted love, sees giving as a weakness, unless you are guaranteed to get in return. Children, this is ridiculous. If you must be assured you will get something in return, you are not giving, but buying, or procuring. Giving must be pure and if you use your time on earth properly, giving and learning about heavenly things, I will teach you to love, and prepare you for the pure grade of love you are destined to experience in the next world. I will enable you, by degrees, to experience My love, which is genuine, and this is the goal and purpose of your time here in the world. Study Me, child. Study Me, and you will learn. You will see your relationships changing. You will see your view of the world changing. You will learn that much of what is called love in this Age of Disobedience, is really exploitation, and not even remotely similar to love. I will open your eyes to a greater degree, and then to a greater degree again, and again, until you see with My eyes. At that time, you will begin to see the need for this change I am bringing about. The more you can see, My small child, the more you will burn to help Me. So work hard on your spiritual duties, little soul, that I may teach you about love.

Friday July 18 2003
Blessed Mother

Often this is an easier lesson for mothers, because mothers usually carry love within. Dear mothers, I speak to you solemnly now. You must be active in protecting your children. Too many mothers have abdicated their responsibilities to the world, as though this modern world could possibly substitute for the love of a mother. This is because of self-love, another current distortion. Yes, children, you must love yourself as a temple of the Holy Spirit and a representative of Christ, but you must not love yourself to the distraction of your duty, your love of others, and your service to the Lord. But this is what I see, and it frustrates me. I say to you, children, that this is wrong. This is a mistake. You must begin again, and learn about love from Us, your heavenly guides. God, your Father, is the best source of the education of love. He created us, His children, in pure love. He created this beautiful world, so that in it we could learn the tuition of love and loving others. He calls us back now to pure love, to heavenly love. Our chosen ones must set the example of love and in this way identify the flaws in what they are practicing and experiencing. Their hearts will begin to melt, and when ice melts, it becomes water. This water, the result of the melting, will nourish the seeds of love God has planted within. A great germination will occur and because these are extraordinary times, this growth will explode into the most beautiful blooms of love. The children of the world today are blessed because of the great opportunity being made available to them. I am with you, dear children. Your mother protects you and will teach you about love.

Friday July 18, 2003
Blessed Mother

My children, move swiftly when you feel called upon to work for Us. Jesus needs many things accomplished and He needs you, His chosen ones, to do this work. The service to My Son is a joyful service and all true freedom lies within this service. You see, little ones, you can serve only one master, and when you stop serving Jesus, you begin to serve the world. That is not what I want for you, my dear one, and not what Jesus needs from you. He needs your loyalty and your action. He needs your duty completed in such a way that there is no question about where your allegiance lies. Be thorough now, children, in the completion of these requests. Many, many souls depend on your answering this call. I am with you and will attempt to keep everything clear for you. Ask for My help when you feel the need and I will assist you.

Saturday July 19, 2003
Jesus

I want to speak to My children about trust. We are practicing trust at this time, because there will come a time in your life when trust will provide you with all manner of comfort and spiritual safety. Indeed, there will come a time when children of the Light will flee to their trust and wrap it around them like a protective blanket. In the time of upheaval, trust in God will come naturally to My chosen souls who have practiced. I am seeking a fullness of union with My children. In this way, service to your God becomes easy. You would not trust someone you did not know, who is a stranger. Therefore, you must come to know Me. Through prayer, you will develop an easiness with Me, despite My divinity. It was never intended that mankind live apart from his God. It is for this reason the world experiences such profound darkness. The world has moved away from My heart. The world is deluded into thinking union with God is unattainable, and even sadder, unimportant. Spirituality and your relationship with the God of All is not something extra, like a hobby. It must be the defining compass in your life, always directing your journey. You need only look around to see the result of living without this love and direction. Man, who professes to be so aware of seeing to himself and addressing His own needs, is starving to death in a loveless wasteland. A person who has a genuine love for himself sees God as his friend, his ally, and loves all those around him. A person who has a genuine love for himself forgets about himself in the service to others. Ponder that thought, children, for in it lies the answer to the universe. I will clarify it for you if you ask Me in prayer. Be happy, dear children, for your Jesus loves you, and guides you with joy.

Saturday July 19 2003
Blessed Mother

I am a good example of trust, dear children of the light. My time on earth was filled with times where a heavenly perspective was necessary. If you view the world from a worldly perspective, you will feel fear quite often. But a heavenly perspective grants peace and emotional security. Trust in God, and in His purpose and will moving in your life, grants you a detachment that liberates your spirit and frees you to do many things. You can relinquish the rush to acquire that has consumed much of the world. Dear children, who have been blessed with great wealth, let go of the material now. It is cluttering your outlook and progress. Remember, you are not bringing these things to heaven, nor will you need these things. They are nothings and should be assigned no value. And if you assign no value to the material things, you will not need to acquire them. It is very simple. The happiest people require little and the more pulled into the quest for things without heavenly value, the more difficult for you to be happy. Your soul seeks bread and you feed it with materialism. This is not the way, my dear little unhappy children. Always compare yourself to those who have less and be grateful. Comparing yourself to those who have more creates envy, and this we must not have. Give your envy to Jesus and He will burn it up in the fires of His Sacred Heart. Away with envy, children. There are reasons you do not have this thing you crave. I am with you and speak with a mother's desire for her children to understand where their unhappiness originates. Little children, step away from material things, so that I can show you the delights of union with my Son. Your mother loves you, and desires your happiness.

Saturday July 19, 2003
Blessed Mother

My dear children, I want to place love in your family. Follow the example of the Holy Family. We were tolerant of each other, as we followed the will of the Father in our lives. We knew that each one of us was an individual, created to serve the Father in our own way. Our goal as a family was to support each other as we gradually discovered the will of the Father in our lives and moved toward our destinies. It must be the same with each of your families. You have been placed with the people around you in order to bring each other closer to Christ and to assist each other in conforming to God's will for you. Be patient with the flaws of your family members, but do not tolerate immorality in your homes. Immorality will destroy your family if you let it go unchecked. Be vigilant about protecting the Spirit of God in your homes. I will help you if you ask me. I will protect your children and guide you away from dangerous and threatening practices. Children, the home is the place where the formation of souls occurs. It must be conducive to spiritual growth and development. Be assured that God watches the events in a home closely. Jesus wants to be part of your family. Treat my Son like the family member He is. Welcome Him into your homes and He will draw you all together and keep you confirmed in grace. When a family member is in spiritual danger,

recommend that person to Jesus and to me and
We will assist in drawing your loved one back to
you. Let the Holy Family be your example and the
graces will flow down upon you and your families. Your mother blesses you and smiles with joy
as she watches you love each other.

Thoughts
on Spirituality
–9–

Sunday July 20, 2003
Blessed Mother

Dear children, walk with the authority of my Son, Jesus Christ. Because you follow Him, you must see things through His eyes and respond to situations with His heart. Now that is different from what you would be doing before you came to follow Him, so it is a change. It is something new. When you begin to do something new, you must do it slowly and carefully, until you gain confidence in yourself and know that you are doing it well. Move slowly in your service to Christ, dear child, as you must take direction along the way. This direction can only come to you if you are listening to my Son as He speaks to you. Dear child, there is really no other way for you. You are a person of good will, therefore you must walk the worldly paths no longer. We will direct your footsteps but you must listen. I know you wish to follow Our heavenly guidance and truly, I say to you, We need you to follow Our direction now. In order to do that you must spend time in prayer. Consider prayer as conversation. You would not begin a strange task without instruction and if you did, you would quite possibly do it incorrectly. Converse with Jesus every day, several times, and you will complete the tasks He chooses for you with perfect purpose. You may then walk away from these tasks, knowing that God's will was accomplished. At times you will see the fruits; at times you will only be sowing the seeds. The fruits will come later, out of your line of vision. Either way, you have completed your portion and can rest easily. Be at peace now on this day as We direct you in the service to your God. I extend my blessing upon you and offer you God's grace.

Monday July 21, 2003
Jesus

My children must ready themselves for spiritual warfare. It is prudent to be prepared when a battle looms before you. In this way, a seasoned soldier remains calm in the fray and resists panic, simply using the skills he has been trained to use. The outcome has been secured, dear children. I, your God, will overcome the enemy of Light and My children will be saved. Still, this battle must be fought and I would have you prepared. How does one prepare, you ask? Of course, you must pray, and pray with discipline, practicing Holy Indifference. Pay no attention to the why behind My requests. It is enough for you to understand what it is I am asking. A soldier does not always need to be apprised of the bigger picture and understands that in time, all will be revealed to him. I am with you. Do not become discouraged when you see the strength of the enemy. I am infinitely stronger. The situation must come to completion, however, and my children of the Light must play their parts. It is for this reason I have placed you where I have placed you, and for this reason I guide you in this way. I am preparing you for the time of the battle, when you will be given the opportunity to serve Me and My

Kingdom. Be joyful to have been chosen as My servant for truly the least of My servants is exalted in heaven, as a child of the Great Goodness. My children hear My voice and truly I call out to them now. Hear My call in your heart as together We begin this journey of love. Be consistent. Be always in the habit of asking Me to reveal My holy will to you and I will do so. It is for this reason I cry out to you. I need soldiers willing to serve in obedience. You must cast off the influence of the world and prepare yourself to be obedient to Me, your God, who seeks to restore this world to goodness and spiritual safety. Your children will experience the world differently and for this you can sing praise to your Creator and offer thanksgiving. Prepare yourself now to serve Me in love and obedience. You will always be glad you chose the side of Light.

Monday July 21, 2003
Blessed Mother

My children, please try to understand what a great grace God has allowed by giving you such loving and specific instruction. Please thank Him for these graces, so that We can continue to guide you in this manner. Your mother is with you, and, like any mother, watches closely to see if her children are developing as they should. I call out to you a motherly warning now. Turn your face away from the world. Many of our great chosen ones spent their whole lives very much in the world, but not of the world. If you are called to do this, do not begrudge us this work. It is for this reason you have been placed in your current position to be the ears, the eyes, the hands, and the heart of Jesus, exactly where you are. Indeed, if more people had been doing this consistently, as they were destined to, the world would be a place of great light and comfort. All of God's children would have food and clean water, and would be living lives of comfort and serenity, as they developed their souls and prepared to move on into the heavenly realm. Alas, this is not the case and your God seeks to cleanse the world and restore His light to every corner of the world. This, however, is a process, like your evolution to holiness, and like your evolution to holiness, it will not be without a degree of hardship and sacrifice. That is what must occur for the light to be restored in your world.

We must be brave, be calm, and be prepared to do our part, with the emphasis on service to God and His divine plan. Dear children, you are blessed to have been called, so do not hesitate or hold back anything from Jesus. You must give and give. I am with you and will remain with you, and truly, no child is fearful when the child's mother hovers nearby. I bless you and extend my hands over you in protection, marking you as my own. God gives me heavenly authority as the mother of the Savior and I use this authority to place myself between each one of my children and darkness. I am the woman clothed with the sun, and I bring God's light to this world, with all of the power of heaven as my weapon. Be at peace, for truly your mother holds before you an impenetrable shield, protecting you from the enemy. Think of this and you will never fear. Call out to me and I will hear you."

Monday afternoon, July 21, 2003
Blessed Mother

My dear children, I wish you to spend time every day considering God's will for you on this day. You must do this in silence. You may have many questions and it is in silence, in your heart, that We can answer these questions. Otherwise, you do not hear Us over the noise of the world. Most of Our children do not hear Us, despite Our attempts to communicate with them. Even many of Our chosen ones neglect this form of contemplative prayer. Children, it is in this prayer that you will find the peace and guidance you require. I want others to see Christ in your face. For this to happen, you must be united with Christ. As always, I bless you and extend my hands over you in love.

Tuesday July 22, 2003
Jesus

Today, I wish to speak to my souls about the love I desire them to have for their fellow man. My children of the Light must think in heavenly terms, as We have said. This means that you should consider your world from My perspective. Within your souls, I cultivate a great love for all of mankind. Do not quash this process. Nurture this love when you feel it because it is work that comes from Me and I am completing it. Feel pity for your brothers and sisters the world over, as I felt pity for the women of Jerusalem. Such suffering you will see when you look at this world from My eyes. There is great hardship, it is true, in the form of sickness and deprivation. But often those souls have their eyes turned to heaven and I am able to console them. Their time in heaven is assured. What is more tragic is the emptiness I see in the more affluent parts of the world. Look into the eyes of your brothers and sisters, dear children. Often you see a flatness, a blankness. Let this move your heart to all manner of compassion because these souls are unloved. No softness or kindness ignites the divine and they have turned cold. This, dear children, is the real tragedy. A whole generation has been lost to affluence. Can you understand why I must respond and remove the affluence that blocks the Light for these souls? Truly, you must all be like children, trusting Me for everything. When a child is put in his bed to rest at night, the child closes his eyes and thinks of peaceful thoughts, related to his mother, father, and his day. He does not lay awake, consumed with the desire to acquire more possessions. He does not lay awake, consumed with worry over how to keep the possessions he has already acquired. My souls in the world must be like children, resting in the knowledge that I will care for their needs and provide for them. I will care for you, dear children. You, in turn, care for My needs, which always have to do with souls. I am placing love in your heart. Ask Me for more and I will send more. Beg Me all during the day to send you love for even the most odious of souls and it shall be yours. In this way, the blankness in the faces of the unloved will disipate, replaced with the look of joy, the look of a soul who has come to life and once again proceeds on a journey to self-knowledge because he has seen love. I am with you and if you read My gospels you will see that I am asking you to do exactly what I did. You are to become like Me. And that is My plan.

Tuesday July 22, 2003
Blessed Mother

Let your hearts exult at this perfect and beautiful heavenly plan. Jesus is all goodness, all kindness, and all love. When I say all love, little ones, I mean that His every action, every motivation, every consideration, originates in love. He calls to you from love. He guides you from love, and often, He corrects you out of love. He sees this world, where the flow of love has been disrupted, and because He loves so deeply and perfectly, He suffers. He grieves. Many souls are lost in this dark time and God has nodded to His angels. Changes are coming. You should pray for these changes and be joyful over them because they are the will of God, who seeks to rescue His children and restore the world to previous beauty and joy. Can you imagine, dear ones, your world with everyone loving God and loving each other? Can you imagine your world where the chief concern is the movement toward holiness and heaven? All will assist each other with the common goal being the transition that occurs in the soul to ready it for eternity in heaven. Children, this is God's plan. The world was like this once and now it is time for the world to return to this state of existence. Be happy, because the hand of the Father is guiding these changes and they are all for the good. Children of the Light, play your part with confidence. If you ask, We will send you a burning desire to see God's will accomplished.

Pray in this way and We will be pleased. I share this little glimpse of God's plan so that you will not be afraid and focus on fear. That is not what We wish. Focus on your holy duty this day, completed in union with Jesus. I bless you, and smile upon you now, as my heart is filled with love and tenderness for you. Be at peace, little soul. Your mother is nearby.

Tuesday July 22, 2003
Blessed Mother

Dear children, it is I, your heavenly mother, who speaks to you today. Do not fear sacrifice. Many of Our chosen souls hold tightly to worldly possessions. It is this last barrier that I seek to penetrate. View material possessions as so many nothings, as I have often said. At times, my little souls, you must see material possessions as something more ominous even than this. You must view them as the baubles of the enemy, with which he seeks to lure you away from the path to Jesus. The less you own, the happier you can be. Do not worry. I will show you what I wish you to have and what I wish you to forgo. If you ask me I will lead you with great care in this matter as it is important. Be filled with joy to be called in this way and together let us remove any barrier that remains between you and my Son. I bless you with joy today as I watch your determined efforts to serve your God.

Wednesday July 23, 2003
Jesus

These words I bring you are more Good News. I want you to share these words as you would share the Good News. If you prepare a great banquet, filled with the finest of foods, you do not sit down alone to sample and enjoy it. You invite friends and loved ones to share and celebrate together. In the same way, I want you to share My words. I will secure the necessary permissions and then you must obey the promptings I place in your heart. All will be seen to. I require only your obedience. I send these words to call humanity back to the Light. I, your God, will move swiftly when the time is right. It is My will that souls be prepared. This is a great mercy of Mine and I would not have humanity treat it lightly. Be assured, dear souls, that I will triumph. My glorious plan is already beginning and if you ask Me, I will remove the blinders from your eyes and awaken your soul from its lassitude with My divine touch. Only ask Me. I call you now and wish to draw you with love into My plan. Respond to Me with all of your energy and love.

Wednesday, July 23, 2003
Blessed Mother

Dear children, Jesus sends you these words of guidance and love as an act of the greatest mercy. Truly, this is a heavenly gift of tremendous proportion. We will make the best use of it and save countless souls. Be holy, dear little chosen souls. Be brave. I have called you to assist on a mission of mercy and I desire your collaboration. For today, be quiet in the knowledge that Our work is about to begin. I bless you and secure every necessary grace for you. When you feel fear, flee to my Immaculate Heart, which will shelter, protect, and sustain you. That is all, my child. You have served Us well in this endeavor.

Wednesday afternoon July 23, 2003
Blessed Mother

My dear children, you may be certain that my favor rests upon you. I am witness to your struggles as you attempt to comply with the will of my Son in your life. You live in a time of darkness and this makes it difficult to be different. Throughout the ages We have called certain souls to advanced or heightened levels of holiness. That is the case now for you, my dear ones. A concentrated effort is necessary to spread the Light, Light that will come to the world through these words. Be assured that you are on the side of victory, despite the apparent strength of darkness. The time is near for my Son to act in such a way that none will doubt His dominion over this world and all humanity inhabiting this world. Many will convert and be saved. We must increase that number through our efforts now. My Son will reveal His will for each of you individually in your hearts. His plan for the world unfolds before you, and in the same way, His plan for each of you will also unfold, in the silence of your hearts, where you must become accustomed to seeking His divine will. Dear children, never be afraid. There is no need. All of heaven stands ready now to do battle for souls. Truly, ask for help and help will come to you. Do not waste these beautiful graces. They are a gift of the most sublime and precious graces available to souls still on earth. I am with you, dear ones. Be happy and hopeful now, as heaven calls out to her children.

Thursday July 24, 2003
Blessed Mother

My children, please welcome the Holy Spirit into your life. You must cultivate this Spirit of God by making your soul an appropriate dwelling place for such goodness. Ask me to intercede for you and I shall. I would like all of my children to pray for the gifts of the Holy Spirit. You will receive these gifts and with them you will serve Jesus. I bless you dear children. My presence dwells near you always.

Appendix

Guidelines for Lay Apostles

As lay apostles of Jesus Christ the Returning King, we agree to perform our basic obligations as practicing Catholics. Additionally, we will adopt the following spiritual practices, as best we can:

1. **Allegiance Prayer** and **Morning Offering**, plus a brief prayer for the Holy Father
2. **Eucharistic Adoration**, one hour per week
3. **Prayer Group Participation**, monthly, at which we pray the Luminous Mysteries of the Holy Rosary and read the monthly message
4. **Monthly Confession**
5. Further, we will follow the example of Jesus Christ as set out in the Holy Scripture, treating all others with His patience and kindness.

Morning Offering

O Jesus, through the Immaculate Heart of Mary, I offer You the prayers, works, joys and sufferings of this day, for all the intentions of Your Sacred Heart, in union with the Holy Sacrifice of the Mass throughout the world, in reparation for my sins, and for the intentions of the Holy Father. Amen.

Allegiance Prayer

Dear God in Heaven, I pledge my allegiance to You. I give You my life, my work and my heart. In turn, give me the grace of obeying Your every direction to the fullest possible extent.

Volume One

Prayer for the Holy Father

Blessed Mother of Jesus, protect Our Holy Father Benedict XVI, and bless all of his intentions.

Five Luminous Mysteries

1. Jesus' Baptism in the Jordan
2. Jesus' Self-Manifestation at the Wedding of Cana
3. Jesus' Proclamation of the Kingdom of God
4. Jesus' Transfiguration
5. Jesus Institutes the Eucharist

Promise from Jesus to His Lay Apostles

May 12, 2005

Your message to souls remains constant. Welcome each soul to the rescue mission. You may assure each lay apostle that just as they concern themselves with My interests, I will concern Myself with theirs. They will be placed in My Sacred Heart and I will defend and protect them. I will also pursue complete conversion of each of their loved ones. So you see, the souls who serve in this rescue mission as My beloved lay apostles will know peace. The world cannot make this promise as only heaven can bestow peace on a soul. This is truly heaven's mission and I call every one of heaven's children to assist Me. You will be well rewarded, My dear ones.

Prayers taken from The Volumes

Prayers to Jesus

"Jesus, I give You my day."

"Jesus, how do You want to use me on this day? You have a willing servant in me, Jesus. Allow me to work for the Kingdom."

"Lord, what can I do today to prepare for Your coming? Direct me, Lord, and I will see to Your wishes."

"Jesus, how do You want to use me?"

"Lord, help me."

"Jesus, what do You think of all this? Jesus what do You want me to do for this soul? Jesus, show me how to bring You into this situation."

"Jesus, love me."

Prayers to God the Father

"What can I do for my Father in heaven?"

"I trust You God. I offer You my pain in the spirit of acceptance and I will serve You in every circumstance."

"God my Father in heaven, You are all mercy. You love me and see my every sin. God, I call on You now as the Merciful Father. Forgive my every sin. Wash away the stains on my soul so that I may once again rest in complete innocence. I trust You, Father in heaven. I rely on You. I thank You. Amen."

"God my Father, calm my spirit and direct my path."

"God, I have made mistakes. I am sorry. I am Your child, though, and seek to be united to You."

"I believe in God. I believe Jesus is calling me. I believe my Blessed Mother has requested my help. Therefore I am going to pray on this day and every day."

"God my Father, help me to understand."

Prayers to the Angels

"Angels from heaven, direct my path."

"Dearest angel guardian, I desire to serve Jesus by remaining at peace. Please obtain for me the graces necessary to maintain His divine peace in my heart."

Prayer for a Struggling Soul

"Angel guardian, thank you for your constant vigil over this soul. Saints in heaven, please assist this dear angel."

Prayers for Children

"Jesus, forgive them."

"Mother Mary, help me to be good."

"God in heaven, You are the Creator of all things. Please send Your graces down upon our world."

"Jesus, I love You."

"Jesus, I offer You my day."

How to Recite the Chaplet of Divine Mercy

The Chaplet of Mercy is recited using ordinary rosary beads of five decades. The Chaplet is preceded by two opening prayers from the Diary of Saint Faustina and followed by a closing prayer.

1. Make the Sign of the Cross

In the name of the Father, and of the Son, and of the Holy Spirit. Amen.

2. Optional Opening Prayers

You expired, Jesus, but the source of life gushed forth for souls, and the ocean of mercy opened up for the whole world. O Fount of Life, unfathomable Divine Mercy, envelop the whole world and empty Yourself out upon us.

O Blood and Water, which gushed forth from the Heart of Jesus as a fountain of Mercy for us, I trust in You!

3. Our Father

Our Father, Who art in heaven, hallowed be Thy name; Thy kingdom come; Thy will be done on earth as it is in heaven. Give us this day our daily bread; and forgive us our trespasses as we forgive those who trespass against us; and lead us not into temptation, but deliver us from evil, Amen.

4. Hail Mary

Hail Mary, full of grace. The Lord is with thee. Blessed art thou amongst women, and blessed is the fruit of thy womb, Jesus. Holy Mary, Mother of God, pray for us sinners, now and at the hour of our death, Amen.

5. The Apostle's Creed

I believe in God, the Father Almighty, Creator of Heaven and earth; and in Jesus Christ, His only Son, Our Lord, Who was conceived by the Holy Spirit, born of the Virgin Mary, suffered under Pontius Pilate, was crucified, died, and was buried. He descended into Hell; the third day He arose again from the dead; He ascended into Heaven, and sits at the right hand of God, the Father Almighty; from thence He shall come to judge the living and the dead. I believe in the Holy Spirit, the holy Catholic Church, the communion of saints, the forgiveness of sins, the resurrection of the body, and life everlasting. Amen.

6. The Eternal Father

Eternal Father, I offer You the Body and Blood, Soul and Divinity of Your Dearly Beloved Son, Our Lord, Jesus Christ, in atonement for our sins and those of the whole world.

7. On the Ten Small Beads of Each Decade

For the sake of His sorrowful Passion, have mercy on us and on the whole world.

8. Repeat for the remaining decades

Saying the "Eternal Father" (6) on the "Our Father" bead and then 10 "For the sake of His sorrowful Passion" (7) on the following "Hail Mary" beads.

9. Conclude with Holy God

Holy God, Holy Mighty One, Holy Immortal One, have mercy on us and on the whole world.

10. Optional Closing Prayer

Eternal God, in whom mercy is endless and the treasury of compassion—inexhaustible, look kindly upon us and increase Your mercy in us, that in difficult moments we might not despair nor become despondent, but with great confidence submit ourselves to Your holy will, which is Love and Mercy itself.

To learn more about the image of The Divine Mercy, the Chaplet of Divine Mercy and the series of revelations given to St. Faustina Kowalska please contact:

Marians of the Immaculate Conception
Stockbridge, Massachusetts 01263
Telephone 800-462-7426
www.marian.org

How to Pray the Rosary

1. Make the Sign of the Cross and say the "Apostles Creed."
2. Say the "Our Father."
3. Say three "Hail Marys."
4. Say the "Glory be to the Father."
5. Announce the First Mystery; then say the "Our Father."
6. Say ten "Hail Marys," while meditating on the Mystery.
7. Say the "Glory be to the Father." After each decade say the following prayer requested by the Blessed Virgin Mary at Fatima: "O my Jesus, forgive us our sins, save us from the fires of hell, lead all souls to Heaven, especially those in most need of Thy mercy."
8. Announce the Second Mystery: then say the "Our Father." Repeat 6 and 7 and continue with the Third, Fourth, and Fifth Mysteries in the same manner.
9. Say the "Hail, Holy Queen" on the medal after the five decades are completed.

As a general rule, depending on the season, the Joyful Mysteries are said on Monday and Saturday; the Sorrowful Mysteries on Tuesday and Friday; the

Glorious Mysteries on Wednesday and Sunday; and
the Luminous Mysteries on Thursday.

Papal Reflections
of the Mysteries

The Joyful Mysteries

The Joyful Mysteries are marked by the joy radiat-
ing from the event of the Incarnation. This is clear
from the very first mystery, the Annunciation,
where Gabriel's greeting to the Virgin of Nazareth
is linked to an invitation to messianic joy: "Rejoice,
Mary." The whole of salvation . . . had led up to this
greeting. (Prayed on Mondays and Saturdays, and
optional on Sundays during Advent and the Christ-
mas Season.)

The Luminous Mysteries

Moving on from the infancy and the hidden life in
Nazareth to the public life of Jesus, our contemplation brings us to those mysteries which may be
called in a special way "mysteries of light." Certainly, the whole mystery of Christ is a mystery of
light. He is the "Light of the world" (John 8:12). Yet
this truth emerges in a special way during the years
of His public life. (Prayed on Thursdays.)

The Sorrowful Mysteries

The Gospels give great prominence to the Sorrowful Mysteries of Christ. From the beginning, Chris-

tian piety, especially during the Lenten devotion of the Way of the Cross, has focused on the individual moments of the Passion, realizing that here is found the culmination of the revelation of God's love and the source of our salvation. (Prayed on Tuesdays and Fridays, and optional on Sundays during Lent.)

The Glorious Mysteries

"The contemplation of Christ's face cannot stop at the image of the Crucified One. He is the Risen One!" The Rosary has always expressed this knowledge born of faith and invited the believer to pass beyond the darkness of the Passion in order to gaze upon Christ's glory in the Resurrection and Ascension. . . . Mary herself would be raised to that same glory in the Assumption. (Prayed on Wednesdays and Sundays.)

From the *Apostolic Letter The Rosary of the Virgin Mary*, Pope John Paul II, Oct. 16, 2002.

Prayers of the Rosary

The Sign of the Cross

In the name of the Father, and of the Son, and of the Holy Spirit. Amen.

The Apostles' Creed

I believe in God, the Father almighty, Creator of heaven and earth. I believe in Jesus Christ, His only Son, our Lord. He was conceived by the power of the Holy Spirit, and born of the Virgin Mary. He suffered under Pontius Pilate, was crucified, died, and was buried. He descended to the dead. On the third day He rose again. He ascended into heaven, and is seated at the right hand of the Father. He will come again to judge the living and the dead. I believe in the Holy Spirit, the holy catholic Church, the communion of saints, the forgiveness of sins, the resurrection of the body, and the life everlasting. Amen.

Our Father

Our Father, who art in heaven; hallowed be Thy name; Thy kingdom come; Thy will be done on earth as it is in heaven. Give us this day our daily bread; and forgive us our trespasses as we forgive those who trespass against us, and lead us not into temptation; but deliver us from evil. Amen.

Hail Mary

Hail Mary, full of grace, the Lord is with you; blessed are you among women, and blessed is the fruit of your womb, Jesus. Holy Mary, Mother of God, pray for us sinners, now and at the hour of our death. Amen.

Glory Be to the Father

Glory be to the Father, and to the Son, and to the Holy Spirit. As it was in the beginning, is now, and ever shall be, world without end. Amen.

Hail Holy Queen

Hail, Holy Queen, Mother of Mercy, our life, our sweetness and our hope, to thee do we cry, poor banished children of Eve; to thee do we send up our sighs, mourning and weeping in this vale of tears; turn, then, most gracious Advocate, thine eyes of mercy towards us, and after this, our exile, show unto us the blessed fruit of thy womb, Jesus. O clement, O loving, O sweet Virgin Mary!

Pray for us, O holy Mother of God, that we may be made worthy of the promises of Christ.

The Mysteries

First Joyful Mystery:
The Annunciation

And when the angel had come to her, he said, "Hail, full of grace, the Lord is with thee. Blessed art thou among women." *(Luke* 1:28)

> One *Our Father*, Ten *Hail Marys*,
> One *Glory Be*, etc.

Fruit of the Mystery: ***Humility***

Second Joyful Mystery:
The Visitation

Elizabeth was filled with the Holy Spirit and cried out in a loud voice: "Blest are you among women and blest is the fruit of your womb."*(Luke* 1:41-42)

> One *Our Father*, Ten *Hail Marys*,
> One *Glory Be*, etc.

Fruit of the Mystery: ***Love of Neighbor***

Third Joyful Mystery:
The Birth of Jesus

She gave birth to her first-born Son and wrapped Him in swaddling clothes and laid Him in a manger, because there was no room for them in the place where travelers lodged. *(Luke* 2:7)

> One *Our Father*, Ten *Hail Marys*,
> One *Glory Be*, etc.

Fruit of the Mystery: ***Poverty***

Fourth Joyful Mystery:
The Presentation

When the day came to purify them according to the law of Moses, the couple brought Him up to Jerusalem so that He could be presented to the Lord, for it is written in the law of the Lord, "Every first-born male shall be consecrated to the Lord."

(Luke 2:22-23)

One *Our Father*, Ten *Hail Marys*,
One *Glory Be*, etc.

Fruit of the Mystery: ***Obedience***

Fifth Joyful Mystery:
Finding the Child Jesus in the Temple

On the third day they came upon Him in the temple sitting in the midst of the teachers, listening to them and asking them questions.   *(Luke 2:46)*

One *Our Father*, Ten *Hail Marys*,
One *Glory Be*, etc.

Fruit of the Mystery: ***Joy in Finding Jesus***

First Luminous Mystery:
Baptism of Jesus

And when Jesus was baptized . . . the heavens were opened and He saw the Spirit of God descending like a dove, and alighting on Him, and lo, a voice from heaven, saying "this is My beloved Son," with whom I am well pleased."   *(Matthew 3:16-17)*

One *Our Father*, Ten *Hail Marys*,
One *Glory Be*, etc.

Fruit of the Mystery: ***Openness to the Holy Spirit***

Second Luminous Mystery:
Wedding at Cana

His mother said to the servants, "Do whatever He tells you." . . . Jesus said to them, "Fill the jars with water." And they filled them up to the brim.

(John 2:5-7)

One Our Father, Ten Hail Marys,
One Glory Be, etc.

Fruit of the Mystery: ***To Jesus through Mary***

Third Luminous Mystery:
Proclaiming the Kingdom

"And preach as you go, saying, 'The kingdom of heaven is at hand.' Heal the sick, raise the dead, cleanse lepers, cast out demons. You received without pay, give without pay." (*Matthew* 10:7-8)

One Our Father, Ten Hail Marys,
One Glory Be, etc.

Fruit of the Mystery: ***Repentance and Trust in God***

Fourth Luminous Mystery:
Transfiguration

And as He was praying, the appearance of His countenance was altered and His raiment become dazzling white. And a voice came out of the cloud saying, "This is My Son, My chosen; listen to Him!

(Luke 9:29, 35)

One Our Father, Ten Hail Marys,
One Glory Be, etc.

Fruit of the Mystery: ***Desire for Holiness***

Fifth Luminous Mystery:
Institution of the Eucharist

And He took bread, and when He had given thanks He broke it and gave it to them, saying, "This is My body which is given for you." . . . And likewise the cup after supper, saying, "This cup which is poured out for you is the new covenant in My blood."

(Luke 22:19-20)

One *Our Father*, Ten *Hail Marys*,
One *Glory Be*, etc.

Fruit of the Mystery: *Adoration*

First Sorrowful Mystery:
The Agony in the Garden

In His anguish He prayed with all the greater intensity, and His sweat became like drops of blood falling to the ground. Then He rose from prayer and came to His disciples, only to find them asleep, exhausted with grief. (*Luke* 22:44-45)

One *Our Father*, Ten *Hail Marys*,
One *Glory Be*, etc.

Fruit of the Mystery: *Sorrow for Sin*

Second Sorrowful Mystery:
The Scourging at the Pillar

Pilate's next move was to take Jesus and have Him scourged. (*John* 19:1)

One *Our Father*, Ten *Hail Marys*,
One *Glory Be*, etc.

Fruit of the Mystery: *Purity*

Third Sorrowful Mystery:
Crowning with Thorns

They stripped off His clothes and wrapped Him in a scarlet military cloak. Weaving a crown out of thorns they fixed it on His head, and stuck a reed in His right hand . . .　　　　(Matthew 27:28-29)

One *Our Father*, Ten *Hail Marys*,
One *Glory Be*, etc.

Fruit of the Mystery: ***Courage***

Fourth Sorrowful Mystery:
Carrying the Cross

. . . carrying the cross by Himself, He went out to what is called the Place of the Skull (in Hebrew, Golgotha).　　　　(*John* 19:17)

One *Our Father*, Ten *Hail Marys*,
One *Glory Be*, etc.

Fruit of the Mystery: ***Patience***

Fifth Sorrowful Mystery:
The Crucifixion

Jesus uttered a loud cry and said, "Father, into Your hands I commend My spirit." After He said this, He expired.　　　　(*Luke* 23:46)

One *Our Father*, Ten *Hail Marys*,
One *Glory Be*, etc.

Fruit of the Mystery: ***Perseverance***

First Glorious Mystery:
The Resurrection

You need not be amazed! You are looking for Jesus of Nazareth, the one who was crucified. He has been raised up; He is not here. See the place where they laid Him." *(Mark* 16:6)

> One *Our Father*, Ten *Hail Marys*,
> One *Glory Be*, etc.

Fruit of the Mystery: ***Faith***

Second Glorious Mystery:
The Ascension

Then, after speaking to them, the Lord Jesus was taken up into Heaven and took His seat at God's right hand. *(Mark* 16:19)

> One *Our Father*, Ten *Hail Marys*,
> One *Glory Be*, etc.

Fruit of the Mystery: ***Hope***

Third Glorious Mystery:
Descent of the Holy Spirit

All were filled with the Holy Spirit. They began to express themselves in foreign tongues and make bold proclamation as the Spirit prompted them.
(Acts 2:4)

> One *Our Father*, Ten *Hail Marys*,
> One *Glory Be*, etc.

Fruit of the Mystery: ***Love of God***

Fourth Glorious Mystery:
The Assumption

You are the glory of Jerusalem . . . you are the splendid boast of our people . . . God is pleased with what you have wrought. May you be blessed by the Lord Almighty forever and ever.

(Judith 15:9-10)

One *Our Father*, Ten *Hail Marys*,
One *Glory Be*, etc.

Fruit of the Mystery: ***Grace of a Happy Death***

Fifth Glorious Mystery:
The Coronation

A great sign appeared in the sky, a woman clothed with the sun, with the moon under her feet, and on her head a crown of twelve stars. *(Revelation* 12:1)

One *Our Father*, Ten *Hail Marys*,
One *Glory Be*, etc.

Fruit of the Mystery: ***Trust in Mary's Intercession***

This book is part of a non-profit mission.
Our Lord has requested that we
spread these words internationally.

Please help us.

If you would like to assist us financially,
please send your tax-deductible contribution to the
address below:

Direction for Our Times
9000 West 81st Street
Justice, Illinois 60458

www.directionforourtimes.com
708-496-9300

Direction for Our Times is a 501(c)(3)
not-for-profit corporation. Contributions are
deductible to the extent provided by law.

Jesus gives Anne a message for the
world on the first of each month.
To receive the monthly messages
you may access our website at
www.directionforourtimes.com
or call us at 708-496-9300
to be placed on our mailing list.

The Volumes

Direction for Our Times
as given to "Anne," a lay apostle

These books are available at
www.directionforourtimes.com
or at your local bookstore.

The *Heaven Speaks* Booklets

Direction for Our Times
as given to "Anne," a lay apostle

These booklet are from the series *Direction for Our Times as given to "Anne," A Lay Apostle*. They are available individually from Direction for Our Times and are listed below:

Heaven Speaks About Abortion
Heaven Speaks About Addictions
Heaven Speaks to Victims of Clerical Abuse
Heaven Speaks to Consecrated Souls
Heaven Speaks About Depression
Heaven Speaks About Divorce
Heaven Speaks to Prisoners
Heaven Speaks to Soldiers
Heaven Speaks About Stress
Heaven Speaks to Young People

New in 2007:

Heaven Speaks to Those Considering Suicide
Heaven Speaks to Those Who Are Away from the Church
Heaven Speaks to Those Who Are Dying
Heaven Speaks to Those Who Do Not Know Jesus
Heaven Speaks to Those Who Experience Tragedy
Heaven Speaks to Those Who Fear Purgatory
Heaven Speaks to Those Who Have Rejected God
Heaven Speaks to Those Who Struggle to Forgive
Heaven Speaks to Those Who Suffer from Financial Need
Heaven Speaks to Parents Who Worry About Their Children's Salvation

More books by Anne, a lay apostle

Climbing the Mountain
By Anne, a lay apostle and Bill Quinn

With great joy, Direction for Our Times introduces the book *Climbing the Mountain*. This soft cover edition contains the fascinating story of how The Returning King Mission began and how it has blossomed into a worldwide apostolate under the watchful eye of and in complete obedience to the Church. Also featured, for the first time in print, is a summary of Anne's mystical experiences of heaven, along with her vision of the call to holiness that each of us must hear.

Inside:
- The story of Anne, wife, mother and lay apostle
- Anne's journey on the Mountain of Holiness
- Anne's experience of heaven
- The entire *Heaven Speaks* collection: Abortion, Addictions, Depression, Divorce, Priests and Religious, Prisoners, Sexual Abuse, Soldiers, Stress, Youths

The Mist of Mercy
By Anne, a lay apostle

Another riveting new book from Anne, a lay apostle. Anne writes in great detail about Spiritual Warfare, and the many subtle and not-so-subtle ways that satan attempts to turn us off the path to holiness. Anne shows how to recognize resistance, and how to quickly overcome it. In Part II, Anne relates her experiences as Jesus takes her to Purgatory and shows her the singular mercies God dispenses to souls who go there. Your views of Purgatory—and of God's merciful justice—will never be the same. This is an uplifting, inspiring work.

Inside:
- How to recognize—and combat—spiritual attacks
- Snapshots of Reality
- Anne's experiences in purgatory
- Monthly Messages of Jesus Christ, The Returning King

Interviews with Anne, a lay apostle

VHS tapes and DVDs featuring Anne, a lay apostle, have been produced by Focus Worldwide Network and can be purchased by visiting our website at www.directionforourtimes.com.